Gandhi — A Prophecy

Gandhi

A Prophecy

B.K. Mallik

PRINTWORLD
Publishers of Indian Traditions

Cataloging in Publication Data — DK
[Courtesy: D.K. Agencies (P) Ltd. <docinfo@dkagencies.com>]

Mallik, Basanta Kumar, 1879-1958.
Gandhi : a prophecy / B.K. Mallik.
p. cm.
Reprint.
ISBN 13: 9788124607558

1. Gandhi, Mahatma, 1869-1948. 2. Statesmen – India – Biography. 3. Nationalists – India – Biography. I. Title.

DDC 954.035092 23

ISBN 13: 978-81-246-0755-8

First published in 1948
by Hall the Publisher Limited, Oxford, UK.

First reprinted in India with fresh typeset in 2014

Printed and published by:
D.K. Printworld (P) Ltd.
Regd. Office: Vedaśrī, F-395, Sudarshan Park
(Metro Station: Ramesh Nagar), New Delhi – 110 015
Phones: (011) 2545 3975, 2546 6019; *Fax*: (011) 2546 5926
e-mail: indology@dkprintworld.com
Website: www.dkprintworld.com

To the spirit of
my Ancestry

Foreword

GANDHI is sometimes described as the greatest man of the twentieth century. Interest in him has never flagged and may even be increasing amongst scholars and activists the world over. Well known are several outstanding protest movements inspired by Gandhian *satyagraha* as of Martin Luther King, Lech Walesa, Vaclav Havel and a host of others less renowned. Green movements have drawn on his critique of industrial, urban and economic aspects of modernization, capitalist or communist. Independent India has always had its quota of Gandhian scholars, NGOs, political activists and social reformers. However despite the government's homage to the Mahatma through various observances and rituals, in no significant sense does Gandhi's spirit inform India's state and society, her economic or industrial policies, or her growing urbanization and consumerism. Despite schemes to alleviate rural poverty or devolve powers to village *panchayat*s the central thrust of the Indian state and its self-definition are and have been focused on modernization.

Basanta Kumar Mallik (1876–1958) spent his formative years in the last quarter of the nineteenth century in Bengal, a leading storm centre of what has been described as the Indian Renaissance, out of which emerged poets, writers, mystics, religious and social reformers, philosophers, and inspired by them, politicians and revolutionaries. Mallik belonged to an old Vaishnava family from Nadia, a part of Bengal that had been home to Chaitanya's *bhakti* and the Nava-Nyaya philosophical movements, and indeed he displayed in himself outstanding qualities of both heart and mind, an acute philosophical intellect combined with a spiritual and poetic sensibility.

Like many of his countrymen Mallik was an ardent admirer of Mahatma Gandhi. He was inspired by Gandhi's faith in *ahimsa* and his untiring quest for non-violentizing (to borrow a phrase from Robert Holmes[1]) conflicts, of which the major two in the India of his time were staged between Indian nationalism and the British Raj, and between the Hindu and Muslim communities. He was also excited by Gandhi's attempt to define India primarily in her own categories, social, moral and cultural, and shared his belief that India's civilization was rooted in her villages. As a philosopher-cum-social thinker Mallik dug even deeper into these concepts, using logical and civilizational analysis which often went beyond Gandhi's stated thoughts and writings. Thus we find him tackling problems of peace and social harmony, or analysing Hindu–Muslim relations (see his *The Individual and the Group*, 1939) in categories which do not appear to be strictly derivative from the Mahatma's. But Mallik believed himself to be essentially engaged in the same pursuits of peace and social harmony and that his theoretical formulations were implicit in Gandhi's. He writes: "what I came to uphold as . . . logical thought was verified to the hilt by action spread over half-a-century in the life of Gandhi."[2] As a meta-historian, therefore, Gandhi's sudden departure before the completion of his life's task was an event that required explanation.

Gandhi: A Prophecy, a slender book put together shortly after Gandhi's death, begins and ends with two stand-alone pieces. It starts with his immediate response to the news of

---

1 Robert L. Holmes, *The Ethics of Nonviolence: Essays by Robert L. Holmes*, ed. Predrag Cicovacki, Bloomsbury, 2013.

2 *Gandhi: A Prophecy* (*GAP*), p. 77.

Gandhi's assassination, the opening chapter "Mahaprasthan" which had been circulated privately amongst his friends, as had the final *"Sravana — The 15th"* written five months earlier on the occasion of India's Independence in 1947. The ideas expressed in both are essentially similar as Mallik asserts in: *GAP*: "My vision of the 15th of Sravana stands, and it stands confirmed by the message of Bapuji."

Thus although Mahaprasthan is indeed an authentic *cri de coeur* uttered in a state of heightened consciousness brought on by intense grief, it is very much a Mallikean statement though made through the medium of (an incorporeal) Gandhi. Interested literary and other scholars may want to analyse the psychic, poetic and other dimensions of Mallik's claims to record what Gandhi is dictating to his mind — but what concerns the reader is the message.

In a short space of about seventy pages the chapters between Mahaprasthan and Sravana provide a brief synoptic of the philosophical-cum-sociological arguments of Mallik's metaphysical tome,[3] easily grasped by close friends familiar with his thought, but a challenge to readers exposed to his thinking for the first time. They could also bear in mind that the philosophical environment in which he lived, whether in Calcutta or Oxford, had a strong presence of British idealism (later overtaken by positivism and analytic philosophy), Hegelianism, and the phenomenon of Marxism whether enshrined in the Communist Party of the Soviet Union which captured power in 1917 — i.e. while Mallik was still reading at Oxford, or the minds of several Bengali intellectuals with whom he interacted in Calcutta in the 1920s and 1930s. The development of atomic physics generated its own excitement in the philosophic world. Mallik's unique metaphysical system reflects his acquaintance with and responses to some of these

[3] *The Real & the Negative* (*RN*), London: George Allen & Unwin, 1940.

ideas and events, interwoven with recognizably Indian structures of thought.

The opening text elaborates on a warning sounded by Gandhi after his death, drawing lessons from his unfulfilled struggle to realize his overreaching goal of "peace in the human home", for Mallik firmly believed that Gandhi desired not only freedom for an undivided India through non-violent means (in which endeavour he experienced frustration), but peace for the whole world, and indeed peace is essentially indivisible. The warning, proclaiming the necessary conditions for successfully achieving not only stable peace, but any ideal an individual may conceive of, is implicitly deduced as it were, from the lessons drawn from his own life.

To better understand the drift of his arguments couched in his particular terminology, one must provide some gloss for a few terms howsoever condensed and inadequate, though there is no substitute for reading his original strictly philosophical work.[4] Some of these key terms are "moral and legal states", "authoritarian and libertarian" societies, and the "society of beings".

In his early works Mallik like many of his contemporaries, saw the post-colonial pre-Cold War world dominated by a struggle between West and East, i.e. between Europe (including the Anglo-Saxon world) and Asia. These he respectively characterized in societal terms as humanistic or individualist societies where all value derives from their constituent individuals, and the group or mystical societies where value resides in the multiple groups, of castes, clans, families, trades, etc. contained within an overall Oneness. (Mallik was to later add a third societal form, the dualist or community type, exemplified by but not confined to the Abrahamic societies, which seek to combine both individual

---

[4] See *RN*.

and group (community) values mediated through a direct relationship with God.)

The societal types along with their economic and state structures embody these opposing and fundamental values, each making an unwarranted leap into ascribing absoluteness to its fundamental preference. This undermines the possibility of coexistence as they are prone to internal and external attempts to reify the supposed universality of their chosen values by winning over or forcibly transforming the internal or external Other through persuasion, absorption, domination, conversion, warfare or at its most worst, elimination through genocide. The pattern of history reflects this competition between opposing societal types, resulting in alternating periods of victory and defeat (at times lasting over centuries) with intervals of impasse or confusion when no value-system clearly dominates. Thus through its imperial project modern humanist Europe expanding from the seventeenth century onwards, suppressed or delegitimized to a greater or larger extent, group (and community) values wherever encountered. In reverse Gandhi in the twentieth-century politically challenged this domination through a demand for national independence to enable the anticipated new Indian state to civilizationally reinstate and re-legitimate received social and cultural values. He was opposed politically by the British, and culturally by Indian modernizers. Mallik always stressed that Gandhi was not for a total return to the past, which was in any case impossible, but for freeing Indians to undertake a creative quest for a genuinely new social paradigm beyond the confines of the Legal and Moral states of history.

Mallik used the term "Legal State" to describe European nations with their Enlightenment ideals of egalitarian individualism, embodied in fundamentally a-religious states where social order and conflicts are mediated through legal processes. Traditional India by contrast relied on the force of social *dharma* for system-maintenance, hence the term Moral State. He did not mean that individuals in the latter were more moral in the ethical sense, but that the order was founded on duties rather than rights, and self-regulated through multiple groups. (He also referred to Indian society as mystical or absorptionist because of its tendency to include multiple and diverse groups in an overarching Oneness.)

Mallik further analysed society as internally divided into at least two camps, both seeking to fulfil the common aims of that society through preferred libertarian or authoritarian means. Thus he saw the Second World War as primarily a struggle between European authoritarianism and libertarianism (or autocratic and democratic states), and each state having its internal competitions, as between parties of the left and right. Similarly the Moral State in India has experienced internal struggles between the Hindus and Buddhists (hierarchists and egalitarians), and similar examples may be found in the other traditional Moral States of Asia.

Such conflicts have been endemic throughout history, and Mallik was convinced that the values which had informed and driven the rival sides, which at times he referred to as "universes" had in the twentieth century "come to grief in the life and death of Gandhi", i.e. finally run out of steam. He now speaks of a "third universe which Gandhi discovered after his death" as the presupposition of the drama of conflict, and also of the advent of the sceptic. This was his reading of India's attainment of Independence and her rejection of Gandhi soon after. If Gandhi successfully opposed the humanistic or Legal State by winning freedom for his country, his desire to substitute it with a rejuvenated Indian model was frustrated by his fellow-countrymen and by the Partition of the country on communal lines.

The word "countrymen" is used advisedly for the opposition to his viewpoint had long been simmering amongst various sections of the population, even amongst Gandhi's colleagues in the Congress party. As Mallik perceptively notes Gandhi was not simply rejected by one individual or group, but the whole country was complicit in the denial not only of peace-making through *satyagraha* or *ahimsa*, but of his entire cultural-cum-social viewpoint (outlined in Gandhi's little classic *Hind Swaraj*). Nehru's own disposition and the preference of the elites for "modernity over tradition", for individualistic humanism either of the right or left, had much earlier led to an undermining of Gandhi's influence within the party, although his moral stature remained tall and unquestioned. The assassination was the culmination of this growing discontent.

The society of beings is a more enigmatic construct, and demonstrates the uniqueness of Mallik as an Indian philosopher who structurally retained certain Indian patterns despite his deep knowledge of and borrowings from the Western philosophic tradition. At the risk of making a broad generalization that Indian philosophy has been basically concerned with individual aporia — psychological, psychical, ethical and epistemological, Western philosophy at least from the days of Plato onwards has in addition concerned itself with problems of the good society, building on the current sociological, cultural and historical analysis. India also had a deep concern with social *dharma*, but the relevant texts were categorized as Smriti or Shastra — more practical treatises on conduct and organization of society than Shruti, roughly translated as intrinsic, abiding and revealed truths. Mallik with his studies of anthropology at Oxford and practical experience of administration in Nepal's ethnically diverse society was more inclined to address socio-political challenges and context them in mutually reflective philosophical and societal constructs, i.e. upgrade if possible, Shastra into Smriti.

He defines society as essentially constituted by individuals-in-relation where individual and group claims have equal value: historically there is no concrete instance of such a societal form. However he inferred from the empirical fact of individuals essentially linked together in groups seeking, with limited success, to define a common aim for their societies and universalize it, a pre-existent group of beings who have already and successfully conceived that common aim, albeit distorted and fractured at the moment of realization. In the historical world as described in GAP, two (to become three) incomplete purposes masquerade as common for all mankind and initiate a continuous process of conflictual interactions.

The simultaneous defeat of both schemes at the mid-point of the twentieth century through India's release from imperial rule and Gandhi's assassination soon after, marks an end to such contentious processes of history. With this "end of history" concept Mallik anticipated Fukuyama's 1992 publication by almost four and half decades, but whereas Fukuyama envisaged the triumphal start of a global reign of liberalism after the demise of the USSR, Mallik declared an end to the domination of all received civilizational forms including liberalism. By this he did not mean that states professing ideological convictions like liberalism or communism would all at once cease to exist, but that all received socio-political forms of organization had irretrievably lost credibility and edge, resulting in widespread confusion and systemic scepticism. The positive side to this lack of absolute conviction is that it would allow for a moratorium on conflict, through his proposed technique of Mutual Abstention. The resulting peace conditions in turn could inaugurate a search for a new social paradigm which would at the least allow a modus vivendi amongst conventional systems before arriving at the genuinely universal. For the search however Mallik lays down stringent rules of procedure which might almost be described as a collective *sadhana*.

Indeed one might say that Mallik shifts to the social plane

the received Indian idea of individual suffering founded in the ignorance of a mistaken sense of self that can be remedied by a *sadhana* of realizing the true Self. He speaks of the need for an "almost religious preparation" to come into touch with the "society of beings" (in later writings capitalized as Society of Beings) through a social discipline which substitutes violence and persuasion by abstention and renunciation, structures the social scheme on absolute equality with regard to the common interest and practices abstention in dealing with conflicting interests.

In an anticipation of Orientalism as the European tendency to project its historical and other schematizations on to the rest of the world Mallik provided an alternative to Western notions of history, particularly with regard to the notion of modernity. . . . Modernity is not, he opined, an a-cultural universal beyond the particularities of Western or Eastern civilization but a new, perhaps more sophisticated restatement of classical European humanism. History moreover moves neither in linear or dialectical progression, but in a series of see–saw movements between opposing socially embedded fundamental values alternately dominating over or losing to one another in refurbished modes of expression. These movements are punctuated not by synthesis but by sheer confusion, and in a sense one might say they have, in their new incarnations, despite the undeniable fact of scientific and technological progress, constantly recycled the same fundamental ideas. (Mallik was to spell this out in greater detail in his 1956 publication, *Non-Absolutes*.) Furthermore his account of history as a record of suffering through periodic frustration and non-fulfilment strikes an almost Buddhistic note, except for the strong focus on societal rather than individual consequences.

As Mallik claims in *Sravana*, the new India about to be born would not revert to either a purely Legal or purely Moral state. "One cannot help being prophetic in the presence of such a re-awakening. My analysis makes it almost scientific certainty."[5] Probably the new Constitution (not ready at Mallik's time of writing) borrowed more from Western "legal" systems than he might have anticipated, and its declared objectives were largely designed to subvert received Indian group society and substitute it with modern Humanism. Individualism was virtually written into the Constitution, although in practice it could not displace the group society in one stroke. But for sure he was correct in discounting the emergence of either a strictly Legal or a Moral state. Perhaps almost by habit, for example, through the (legal) electoral democratic process, the Indian group society has resisted radical individualism through bloc-voting and group-based parties, but yielded to egalitarianism in exercising the power options available to hitherto oppressed or marginalized groups. This rebalancing of hierarchy and privilege is a work-in-progress, lacks precision and clarity, and is not without hiccups and tensions.

Mallik's own ideal, which he also projected as Gandhi's, is not the simple re-establishment of the pre-colonial state, nor an all-out imitation of Western humanism, nor a mixture of the two. Rather his analysis led him to the desirability of a new state altogether different from the Legal and the Moral, which would initiate a move towards a genuine world state.

In other words he appropriated the Marxist–Hegelian prophecy of Utopia, itself the secularization of an Abrahamic concept, but made it fully inclusive, demonizing neither classes nor unbelievers, but placing it in an as yet-to-be-fully-understood category. Such a utopian vision though not immediately or practically realizable, can serve as a limit-concept or ideal to be asymptotically approached. Today the

---

5 *GAP*, p. 90.

weakening of received ideologies and faiths (to which fundamentalisms reflect a desperate reaction) the growing tiredness with overt and covert warfare along with the increasing interconnectedness of the globe and the felt need for an international system (despite discomfort with the idea of a premature world state reflecting skewed rather than genuinely world interests), all point back to Mallik's description of the "post-historical" era — and move forwards toward a collective striving to bury old absolutes (i.e. all received fundamentalisms including secular fundamentalism) and evolving a system of coexistence through mutual abstention — the *sine qua non* for the emergence of a genuinely universal common purpose and a global structure to contain it.

Madhuri Santanam Sondhi

Grateful thanks are due to Susheel Mittal of DK Printworld for his exemplary patience and co-operation in republishing this book. I have received unfailing encouragement from Professors Purushottama Billimoria and Nirmalya Narayan Chakraborty, and am deeply indebted to Mallik's late British disciples Winifred Lewis and Mary M. Walker for their dedication in maintaining Mallik's legacy. I also thank Madhu Chowdhury who empathetically entered into the spirit of Mallik's Mahaprasthan in designing the cover.

Madhuri Santanam Sondhi is author of *The Making of Peace: A Logical and Societal Framework according to Basanta Kumar Mallik* (1985) and *Martin Buber and Basanta Kumar Mallik: An Intercivilizational Dialogue on Peace* (2008). She co-edited with Mary M. Walker *Ecology, Culture & Philosophy: Metaphysical Perspectives from Basanta Kumar Mallik* (1988).

Contents

PART ONE
Mahaprasthan

Mahaprasthan

To any Indian, if he has not deviated from his own tradition, the sudden dramatic exit of Gandhi, however enigmatic its form, must appear as cosmic; it marks at least the end of a phase in a classic tradition of our race which began with Buddha and Mahavir and has periodically surged through all the ages in the proportion of varied themes no bigger than what Nanak, Kabir, Chaitanya and many others gave it. To assess its significance or to commemorate it at this unusual moment is neither a call of duty nor a privilege, however sacred, which any of us can fulfil. Personally, I felt a cord suddenly snap in me as the last rites were done to him on the banks of the Yamuna, and the eternal flames of the Vedic sacrifices took his soul back whence it came. Could I ever cease to feel that he gave his life for us, so that we may live for evermore!

The exit was literally a bolt from the blue heavens; but the wrath that sought it relentlessly may have its roots too far back in the coils of history which time devises to give history a shape. One may never succeed in tracing those roots, so that the issue of appraisal or judgement of the deed that brought it about can with difficulty be faced. Perhaps it would be one small tribute to the memory of our beloved Bapuji if we dropped it altogether and for good. The main issue is to complete the work which was cut short by his death, so that the less we think of punishment for the deed itself as if to expiate a sin or to vindicate the claims of the State, the better would it be for us on whom devolves the clear duty of guaranteeing peace to his soul.

But can we with any conscience pick up the thread of action where Bapuji left it and begin seriously to build before we have taken to heart the deep lessons which this almost diabolic event in our history dictates to us? The lessons are meant for us all, the community at large, since the stakes involved concern our whole heritage rather than a mere technique or a reassertion of a dogma or doctrine which serves only to support our faith as a pillar does a roof. The fact is that we stand to lose today the whole fabric of our faith if perchance we let the emotions, whether of anger or of shame, dictate our policy or make us ruthlessly fasten the guilt on the heads of whole groups or movements which make up our home. If we have to consider the issue of guilt, it may be wiser if we spread it out over the whole community and as a people conscientiously undergo a purification of soul. The main issue, however, is one neither of justice nor even of purification; it is that of taking to heart the fact that we are on the eve of a cataclysmic change in our history. We have solemnly to make up our minds whether we will, with heads bent, tread the path of history if only to fulfil its mission, or will rather choose to leave it for the wilderness which surrounds it. It has to be firmly kept in mind that we descended from an ancient historic stock and have inherited centuries of breeding; that stock and heritage alone holds the mandate for us. It is open to us always to solve the riddle which it left unsolved, but we shall not be suffered to tamper with its integrity, not even for a moment. It is our opponent who belongs to the opposite faith who holds that right by a cosmic fiat, and not the children of the soil. It is for them to preserve the faith and heritage scrupulously against attack, so long as they have not seen fresh light to solve the riddles left behind.

But what exactly are the lessons which Bapuji left for us

by his death? What indeed does his sudden and hurried departure mean? Why did he leave at all? Why do great minds leave when it is their leadership more than anything else in the world that is needed? By common consent the field of history is the only field of action. How could the man of action survive unless there were room for him to act, serve and assuage the pangs of the human heart? What does it mean that at such a tense, precarious moment of our history our Bapuji, whose whole soul was bound up with our welfare and good, should suddenly, and without even a gesture from the heavens, leave us? Life for centuries has been difficult enough; what sense was there to make it even more difficult and leave us to toss on uncharted seas? One may be forgiven for such aberrations of grief; one finds it very hard indeed to forgo the blessings once they have been delivered to us. And will anybody deny that our Bapuji was a rare blessing to us for which the rest of our history will ring for ever and ever with joy and a heart full of thankfulness?

But the lessons, as one reads them, are grim. We inherit from them a legacy which sounds a note of warning. Life is good indeed, but it offers one nothing but varied chances of living, even to the point of being left stripped and naked. Only those who are prepared to find goodness in the heart of discipline and dire penance may survive. Others who seek shelter and avoid the hot midday sun literally die.

I have not been able to find anything but a note of warning in the message which rose steady and straight with the smoke of the funeral pyre. It is human to break, to see all that unblemished purity and wholehearted faith yielding to death as the bird with the rare plumage yields to the gun. Could one believe that this tower of strength that was built on the foundations of ages should ever fall?

The warning is that whatever purpose one may follow and however one may guard oneself with even divine sustenance, there is no certainty whatever about the success of one's aims. No aim or objective, however sacrosanct, is safe. You may profess love, peace and goodwill to men and to all creatures on earth and dedicate your life to them, but the chances are even that your neighbour to whom you offer it may reject it and strike you dead. What you hold honestly and unswervingly to be peace and love, as the very sap of life, may wither your neighbour and kill him outright, as the hot sun withers the tender plant. Why this should be so is quite another question, but it is so, and all the seers and thinkers knew it. History is but one long evidence proclaiming this tale.

There were many instances when Bapuji openly regretted the mistakes and blunders that he made. There was no occasion when he claimed perfection for himself or an unerring comprehension of truth. The light in him on which he lived wavered at times, and he knew it. But his death is the last, final confession that truth is difficult to reach; that no penance is strong enough to guarantee the fulfilment of that journey. No matter what you do and where you are, all have to come to the same confession sooner or later. Most certainly, it is not success or fulfilment of a programme of life that should be one's legitimate aim; perhaps it is, at times, in frustration, its direct opposite, that the clue may be found. Here is, if you like, an enigma for those who value man's intellect to probe the secret of truth and a warning for those who prefer to live by faith. To me the message of our Bapuji's death holds a warning, and I shall try to see what it really means.

It seems to me that there are at least four clear implications which the note of warning I have just broadly stated is pointing to; and what is more to the purpose, they seem to imply a whole structure of life which may be taken as the last and final gift that Bapuji left for us by his death, if we can discover it.

It is here indeed in these clear implications that his last comment on history or tradition will be found; and perhaps, also, the fruition of his long-drawn-out discipline which ended like a ritualistic sacrifice of life. How the Shades of Vedic tradition follow us! No doubt even to the cynic, our debt to him knows no bounds. What he achieved in his lifetime was not within the dream of any countryman or woman of ours, however gifted, even as a plan or an ideal. If today, once again after long centuries, the fresh pure air of independence is sweeping over the mountains and the limitless plains of our ancient land, it is chiefly because our Bapuji by persistent sacrifices and privations lifted us out of bondage. But while this unrivalled achievement classed him with all those martyrs who gave their lives for their motherland, it was but an episode or detail in his plan, the object of which was to bring peace to the human home, to make men love one another, to make them live together in peace instead of living apart or in a state of perpetual discord and clash. And it is this fulfilment that is implied by the gift which he has left by his death which holds a note of warning, with positive implications about the future home of man.

To me with solemn assurance this note of warning has a core in it, and in that core there is a nucleus. It is what this nucleus stands for that is left to us as his last precious gift. The lessons as we read them do not contain this nucleus; they tell us no doubt the truth, but this is not the whole truth, nor the truth which I take it dawned on Bapuji just as the fates decided that he should wind up the long career of penance and sacrifice. It is as if today our Bapuji is once again gathering up all to his side and making for our benefit a comment on history to serve as the total meaning of all that he went through under the direct guidance of his beloved faith. Here in the nucleus of the warning is a prophecy for the age that is coming, a message which fell due as the rigour of asceticism and the abandonment in love for the whole of mankind made a way for it into the human heart. Not before he put himself to the test of the severest discipline and walked the path of rectitude and single-minded purpose with head erect was he in a position to hold that message. Nor, perhaps, were we who are left behind in a position to receive it from him until grief for his death consumed all the dross out of our soul. Our tradition set it almost as an adage that those who follow the masters have to read solemnly the meaning of the message they left behind. What follows, once the message has been delivered, is only an attempt to comprehend the truth, to formulate it or to interpret it, as our thinkers call it. If perchance we are blessed today with the clean and pure spirit which grief alone grants us, we shall see the meaning of the message which our Bapuji left as a prophecy in the nucleus which forms the core of that warning, which sounded so audibly in the flames as they took his soul away.

The comment as I read it with bowed head opens out with four distinct notes. I shall state them as they sound to me, one by one.

The first, as it comes to me, can almost be inscribed on stone. No matter what provision anyone can make to assure themselves about an ideal or plan, the process of assurance is never complete till it has been sanctified by acceptance inspired by consent alone. Those who offer gifts, whatever their own conviction, have to wait on the receiver of those gifts to test them with his own conviction. To make a gift is just as much an obligation as to receive one, even as the capacity to fulfil the obligation is hard to earn. A gift, again, can never be offered unless there is an occasion for receiving it, exactly as there can be no receiving of a gift if there was no offer made. The giver and receiver of gifts imply one another and normally appear together. A society has no meaning which does not make provision for both, and there is no society in which both the giving and receiving of gifts do not occur.

And yet this simple phenomenon of our life has its roots in the very foundation of our social home. The giver of gifts in common parlance is the man or woman who formulates an ideal and works out a scheme or plan, whilst the receiver of the gift is the one who assimilates or works the ideal or plan into the texture of our social scheme. They function differently, and fashion the two main interests of the society in two distinct phases of it. In terms of analogy, the two functions are, for instance, like making sugar and building up the bones with it or going through the whole process of composing a music and equipping oneself for hearing it. Logically, they imply the thesis that all process or activity, whatever its form is dual by nature, in the sense that there is an active as well as a passive form of it. While the main objective is singular and monistic, its realization necessarily implies a dual function. That is one reason why our sense-organs have both the active and passive forms.

But even apart from all this technical evidence the simple elementary fact stands out, that the giver of the gift is not the judge of the relevancy or the suitability of the gift he offers. There is no a priori or prima facie evidence by which it can be tested or verified. The body, alone, by digesting the sugar can testify to the soundness of its manufacture. It is for the audience to say whether there was music in the composition. There is such a thing as assimilation of a plan or scheme into the texture of society, or the art of making a theory or plan or scheme live in the body politic. And whatever testing goes into the stage of preparing or formulating the ideal or plan — it may be seeking the aid of scholarship with fresh analysis, or of rigid ascetic practices, supplemented by divine aid to illumine the core of the ideal — all that goes to determine the choice of the ideal and doctrine itself. It is only the thinker or seer who forms his choice by such testing, and who then proceeds to preach and propound it to the community at large. It has nothing whatever to do with the process that leads to its verification or assimilation, or the realization of the ideal. The giver of the gift, or the preacher, or the seer is still wholly dependent on the verdict of the community, whether it is acceptable to them or not, whether indeed it admits of being fashioned into a living principle.

And if we admit acceptance by consent, as at least one of the tests for validating the soundness of the scheme or ideal, it follows that Gandhi's offer of love and peace had to wait for the acceptance and consent of those to whom he offered them. He was wholly dependent, for instance, on an Englishman like Winston Churchill, or a Moslem like Muhammed Ali Jinnah, or a Hindu like the Mahratta brahmin, for assimilating this love into the texture of the social scheme to which they belonged. At any rate, Gandhi must have faced that specific issue, whether he was fully aware of its implications or not; and the course of events which followed after the offer was repeatedly made, would bear analysis if we reviewed it in the light of the doctrine of consent I have just formulated. There is no occasion to raise a mere historical issue.

The point however which deserves close and careful analysis refers to the bearing of this doctrine on Gandhi's own theory of non-violence. May we not think that this doctrine of consent not only coincides with the theory of non-violence, but perhaps suggests a definition of that much-disputed term "violence"? If, for instance, the term "consent" is distinguished from the term "authority", violence and non-violence could in that case be identified with "authority" and "consent". At this rate, those who claimed that a doctrine or theory could be established wholly on a priori evidence, and repudiated the necessity of verification or consent could be regarded as advocates of violence, while the others, who made consent the *sine qua non* of verifiability, would belong to the school of non-violence.

It is quite another story whether the doctrine of non-violence was actually formulated by Gandhi in this specific form. In any case, I am not in a position to discuss that point, nor am I interested in it. If, however, he did hold such a view in some form or other, there could be no occasion for him either to impose his doctrine of love by force on others or to try even to persuade them to believe that his was the only true doctrine. On the contrary, his main function would lie wholly in simply formulating his doctrine, hoping that it would be worked into the texture of the social scheme. His right to preach and formulate would remain, but there would be an obligation on his part to recognize an equal right to accept or consent on the part of his fellow men and women. Violence and non-violence, according to this view, have nothing whatever to do with persuasion and force: since the issue between persuasion and force is the issue between two kinds or types of energy and force.

I do not, however, suggest any comment on what Gandhi did or did not mean by his doctrine of non-violence; in fact I am keeping clear of any reference to his thoughts and deeds during the years when he was with us in the flesh and moved with us in what we call the arena of life. I am not even writing a memorial to him, but am just recording what he seems to be dictating to my mind. There is no reason to discuss whether I am making a myth of his personality or laying in a store of material for a future legend. But I have not the slightest doubt that all that I am saying about him is true in some sense or other. There is a clear connection between my experience of him at the moment and the life that passed away for good the other day on the banks of the Yamuna. Whether the doctrine of *karma* would give support to it, or some deep law of continuity would account for it, is more than I am prepared at the moment to discuss. It is very difficult to trace the lineage of the occult, visionary or legendary in human history; for some at least do not see any evidence to distinguish between the verifiable and the legendary from the point of view of what we call truth — all such issues are problems created by the human mind as a matter of course, as if to fill in the gaps. There is sufficient evidence in history to make us realize that so far in human history there has been nothing but a fight between illusions, with intervals of rest in the exhaustion of doubt. And the account that I am giving of Gandhi refers to the period which began after we took special care to give him the chance of dying like a martyr and a suitable mourning to wind up that shameful record in our history. It is neither here nor there to ask whether the Gandhi of my experience at the moment is literally the same figure who lived and died the other day. It is not necessary to deny that there is such a phenomenon as death. But it does not follow that because death strikes us, so that we have to leave the known haunts of our earthly life for good, there may not be chances for us to wake up from death as from a slumber, and find ourselves in the stream of life that is the universe. The point to note is that if death meant extinction, one single instance of it would have spelt disaster for the universe at large, since no life ever existed in an isolated state, but in deep interrelation with other lives. I have every reason to believe that I am not dealing with fiction when I am recording my experiences with our Bapuji, though I am least able to advise my friends as to how they should cultivate the companionship as I am doing. One cardinal fact, however, I shall mention which would give at any rate a virtual support to my claim that our Bapuji is alive and dictating his comment on history as he never had the chance of doing in his late life on earth.

If we are precise in our thoughts we have to admit that

the experiment of our Bapuji for fifty long years in the heart of what we call the modern age embodied the last experiment in the most jealously guarded tradition of the human race. And if at the end nothing remained of it but the ashes which today we are depositing in the soil again so that life may spring up, may we not conclude that we have seen in this collapse the end of the trail of conflict in which we groped about ever since we were born? The drama of which Gandhi was the hero was not the drama in which any of our prophets took part. There was no sign of it, even when Buddha and Mahavir appeared. Even while only the other day Ramakrishna trod the same path in the essential forms as Gandhiji did, the experiment in tradition was still being made with success. It had goodness in it sufficient to produce the conviction that it was possible to reach truth and light, so that we might not fall into darkness again. But only smoke arose when the fifty years' penance was completed, only ashes were left behind; so that now we could go on a pilgrimage with a clear mind and clear conscience. And the fire that consumed that experiment in its fiftieth year was ignited as if by a passing wind. The guides of values and wisdom disappeared; in the darkness that followed there was only one direction left and that was the sense of bafflement for one and all.

Could I then not claim that the hero of this drama of bafflement had a right by nature to what was bound to follow in its trail? If the whole of this drama was embodied in Gandhi more than in any other figure of history, did he not stand out as the heir-apparent to all that was destined to follow? In some sense or other it has to be granted that he is surviving; and that assurance is enough for me to believe that I am recording his comments on the universe.

It is time for me however to record the second note of the comment which by its firmness and precision stands as the edicts in our history did!

No matter what pains we may ever take to escape it, there is no power on earth or in the heavens which can save us from frustration of purpose, if perchance our purposes happen to stand opposed by others.

If it is impossible that we can act without a purpose, obstacle or opposition to purpose can mean only disaster to it sooner or later. There is only one condition which can guarantee realization, and that is absence of opposition, or as we call it, harmony. In harmony, purposes are supposed to coincide and the creatures who cherish them to co-operate. But once the relation between them changes into opposition, or when they do become direct opposites, the fates decree that they should meet with complete and utter frustration. There is no alternative to it.

It is another story, however, whether purposes, as a matter of fact, do clash and oppose one another, or whether in the nature of things all purposes that are human in conception must be contraries or contradictories, in a state of perpetual conflict. We shall soon have to review this central issue of social relationship. What this comment emphasizes is that there is such a thing as opposition between human purposes, and when that happens, frustration is the only result. In other words, opposition cannot, in the nature of things, be overcome or resolved, however we may desire to overcome it and exert ourselves proportionately to that end.

The theory or principle, however, which lies at the back of the fact that frustration is inevitable is derived from the nature of conflict as such. In so far as conflict, as distinct from harmony, runs through two alternate stages of contradiction and contrariety, purposes which are tied up in conflict suffer as contradictories and contraries usually do. Naturally, they have to share the fate of frustration which falls to the lot of contradictories like the stroke of destiny.

If unity and independence, therefore, clash as contradictories they are bound to meet with frustration as a matter of course. If Gandhi and Muhammad Ali Jinnah, for instance, stood as advocates for unity and independence, nothing could possibly prevent them from standing out as contradictories in open clash. Frustration of their purposes was a foregone conclusion. It was impossible that either of them should realize his purpose. Neither the ideal of unity nor that of independence could be realized. That follows from the nature of the contradictories.

And if, as a matter of fact, such a phenomenon as the partition of India took place, creating the impression that Independence was achieved and opposition to it from the ideal of unity was actually overcome, that was no evidence that the ideal of indepenence escaped frustration for good. It only proved that the ideal of unity was frustrated; there was no guarantee in the Partition that Muhammad Ali Jinnah did or could achieve Independence. There was only evidence in it that he did succeed in frustrating Mahatma Gandhi. Besides, both on grounds of logic and history, the future is holding similar frustration for Muhammad Ali Jinnah and his successors and that inevitably at the hands of the successors of Mahatma Gandhi. And this would mean that the community which he has succeeded in mobilizing for the purpose of frustrating Mahatma Gandhi's ideal of unity would be drawn back within the compass of the Indian society where it had lain for centuries.

Yet, the simple logical point about the contradictories is that they undergo frustration one after the other; when unity, for instance, is frustrated, it suffers that unerring fate at the hands of the protagonists of freedom. At this stage, obviously, it is not independence that is frustrated but its direct opposite, the ideal of unity.

Besides, for Muhammad Ali Jinnah and his Moslem League to be able to frustrate Mahatma Gandhi and Jawaharlal Nehru is not to achieve the ideal of independence as I have already mentioned. The ideal of independence still remains unrealized. What has been realized by them is a freedom from bondage to which they were subject at the hands of the Hindus. That freedom is potent enough to guarantee a temporary respite for the Moslem League and the chances of frustrating the ideal of unity of Mahatma Gandhi and Jawaharlal Nehru. But there is no evidence in this interlude in Mohammedan life of the realization of the ideal of independence. The next stage is set inexorably for the frustration of Muhammad Ali Jinnah's idea of independence. By the Law of the contradictories nothing else can happen, and this will mean the fall of the Pakistan State and the restoration of the Indian unity which the Partition for the time being broke up. Whether it will be good for either the Hindu or the Mohammedan is another question or a different story.

By the same Law again, the incalculable harm done to life and property as a direct result of the Partition and all which came to a head in what has been called "the plucking the flower of life from earth" will be made good by an equally severe nemesis for the Moslem League whether the Hindu or the Mohammedan in either community want it or not. It was not for nothing that millions gave their lives and went through what is called "the hell of agonizing mind" for the achievement of what is called freedom from bondage or the ideal of unity. Such ordeals are gone through since there is no other alternative; and the only solace which history has so far offered has taken the shape of restitution of claims and dues on the basis of justice, which never failed. Yet, I am not exactly quoting from the law of retribution or the "inevitable turn of the wheel"; there is no malice or spite in the spirit of history or in the universe that stages such severe laws which make one and all pay in the name of justice. I am drawing upon the historic lesson which was epitomized only the other day in the life of our Bapuji. Our opponents should realize the enormity of what has happened in the world today, what loss it has suffered in its vitality and strength. Can it ever be that one will escape the nemesis if one has been, even with best of motives and intentions, involved in it — when today at least half the world is mourning the loss of the only soul which kept the light from the heavens shining? Could it possibly mean that the forces and factors which caused that mourning, whatever their goal, could escape exactly such an ordeal when their turn arrives? Why should our opponents have to lose the chances of discipline in the name of justice? Why should we alone have to leave the world, the only place where we sang the songs and cried our hearts out as the last remains of our dearly beloved were cast to the flames? Could not our opponents join us in this pilgrimage and feel in their bones, as we have done, what it is to grieve? The gospel of love is lying in mutilated grandeur, as perhaps the most resplendent fiction of the human mind. What rules inexorably in its place is the Law of Conflict or the Law of Contradictories. Neither the gospel of love nor the gospel of freedom can escape the "law of nemesis", if we go by history alone. The fact of history is that we either suffer from destitution or liberate ourselves from bondage. We never reach our goal, whether it is one of unity or freedom.

The third comment is that no matter what we may do to eliminate suffering from our life there is never any escape from it. Suffering is indelibly stamped as a permanent feature of life as we know it. We voluntarily or involuntarily either create suffering or of necessity fall a victim to it. There is no individual or group which does not have to go through the experiences of suffering and there is no alternative to it.

The principle underlying this comment is that the values

and objectives which we are bound to cherish as we live are at bottom strictly dual in their form. There is no standard or value which is or can be absolute. Even what is called the standard of the absolute is faced by what is called the standard of the relative. In philosophic parlance we call them by the names of the mystical and humanistic, or the authoritarian and libertarian. Besides, so far as our history and tradition go this dichotomy, as a matter of course, has incompatibility in its core. The values clash with one another and have so far lain in a state of continuous opposition. And since conflict took ultimately the form of the contradictories and contraries, what we call suffering arose in the stage of contradiction, a stage in which one side inflicted "suffering" on the other, while the other side simply went through it. There was invariably a turn of the tide.

The fourth comment is that no matter what we may do we cannot possibly escape the universe which has made this life of conflict inevitable. There is no other universe which can give us a shelter from the rigour of the one to which we belong. We are born in it and die in it — perhaps to be born again, if only to die.

Our universe, therefore, while it has produced nothing but negative existence in the form of frustration and suffering is sufficiently positive to produce the illusions which alone could create that negative state. It gives us ample opportunity to act; it is not a universe which ever bred inaction or fruitless rest. Even while it puts us into the mood of despair, and reduces us to a moribund sloth or drives us to the agony of suspense and doubt, it never rules out experience altogether. We always act either to submit or to conquer and never have a chance to fall asleep and forget to face the pangs of suffering. Even our dreams and fictions only add to the variety of this drama. They do not dispute the claims of what we call fact when we feel convinced that we touch the rock bottom of the real. Even if it is only the probable that is verified by what we call fact, fictions and dreams leave even such moments of our experience untouched. But nothing happens whether we are in the land of fiction or dream, or proudly explore the realm of facts, which can be taken as an escape from frustration and pain. The values and objectives remain equally unfulfilled. Our theories and schemes whether in the land of fiction and dreams, or in what we call broad daylight, are verified only for a time when it is our time or turn to inflict suffering on others. Invariably they not only cease to be verified, but are openly and flatly contradicted as soon as it falls due that the other side should prevail.

These are the comments on history which came to me, as it were, through the mouth of our Bapuji. No other individual had the same right or opportunity to make them. That at any rate is my presumption. The period of life that he spent on the earth, the way in which he spent it and the manner in which it received its quietus form the evidences by which the comments stand. The moral law and divine guidance never had a chance of fulfilment more assured and guaranteed.

These are days of furious and stupendous testing; a claim to truth today has to be vindicated and verified, whatever its pedigree or origin. If anything stands firmly in the modern age, it is the crucible of proof. And if there is catholicity of spirit — as perhaps there never was before — naïveté and simplicity, grown to maturity in the soil of fertile humility, are not its *sine qua non* or proof. It is robust enough to face any climb; but the god who suddenly appears on the last ledge of the peak to bless his pilgrims with divine beneficence has to prove his *bona fides* first. This may sound unholy and false to the esoteric mind, but the mind of man today will not have its dignity clouded even by the grace of divinity. If divine presence has to be claimed in the heart of the universe, such a claim can only arise from the heart of human dignity. No god can simply overrule man, just as it will be stupid for man to discard his innate divinity. The test must be there to guarantee the credibility of anything we hold.

Our Bapuji's life was one sustained experience of this test. It never wavered.

There was no myth or legend or vision that was not on trial exactly as the moral law or the Doctrine of Peace and Love. If God truly lived in the heavens and looked after his creation on earth, here was a chance for him to make good his claim. The law that he laid down for divine sustenance was strictly obeyed. Nothing was prayed for or asked for as a matter of grace. The dues were paid to the full. If in spite of that fulfilment on man's part, the message was not delivered and peace did not reign on earth, not only man, but God and the law suffered equally. Both failed the test.

Gandhi's life to me stands out as the main test of the modern age; the object of this experiment was tradition itself, the meaning of life on earth. If God or any man was honest he was: and honesty, to say the least of it, is the heart of all experiment. If there was ever anything impersonal or truly objective, it was the spirit of experiment. It is the latest trail mankind has chosen to tread, and what results are waiting to be born from our Bapuji's experiment it will soon be my effort to formulate as a tribute to the Soul that is gone for the moment.

PART TWO

A Prophecy

I

Legal and Moral Values

The comments I have just recorded on behalf of Gandhiji have never left me ever since they entered my mind; and if I have anything further to suggest with regard to them, it is just a simple and dispassionate analysis of their obvious and hidden implications.

Perhaps I ought to mention that my life with Bapuji was like a drop in the ocean compared to what many leading minds and millions of humble folk today rightfully claim. I had not the chance of sitting at his feet like so many others to assimilate the truth as he quietly spoke it; nor did I ever discuss with him the bastion of his deep faith in the sanity of this universe.

A great portion of my life was spent abroad during the time Gandhiji was giving shape to our political life. Mine was wholly a life of research in the quest of truth. I had to follow the line which our tradition conscientiously set for the students of learning. I moved in a sphere which was distant and remote from the life of our Bapuji.

And so, altogether, I met Gandhiji only twice — once in 1925 when an English friend of mine from Balliol, T.W. Harries and I went to see him, if only to feel his presence, at C.R. Das's house, in Calcutta. That friend died soon after while he was staying with me, and Bapuji's mourning for his sudden death took the shape of a very affectionate reference to it in his paper *Harijan*. The only other time I met him was when he stayed with some relations of mine at Hazaribagh in Bihar. Both Mira Ben and Muriel Lester were with him at the time, and I was in charge of the white-coated goat that gave her milk to him in the early dawn. There were great crowds gathering and ungathering during that weekend, and I shall never forget how he told me repeatedly that the old families of Bengal filled him with great pride, as he found devotion and beauty in perfect equipoise in such homes.

My touch of his personality was very slender indeed, and it may well be asked why I should claim the privilege of recording his comments on history, or of offering an interpretation of them. There is or can be no answer to such a question. What, however, may be permitted as an apology may somewhat retrieve my claim. The fact is that the finale of Gandhiji's life-long experiment marked to me a singular verification of what I had come to uphold in the speculative field. I could not conceive of a more thorough vindication of my claim about the achievement of history which I had already recorded in my Metaphysic; nor was there any other figure in human history to whom I could refer for such a confirmation. It was as if human civilization after its birth in the ancient land of India 6,000 years ago suddenly chose to write its epitaph on 30 January 1948, the day of Gandhiji's death. I have to repeat that the death of Bapuji was not like any other death in human history since it literally marked the close of what we have so far called history or civilization. This may sound strange, but in him died history and that part of the universe which staged that history.

Still, this humble attempt on my part to interpret the comments our Bapuji made has no pretence whatsoever to question any review of his life, not certainly the claim to find a place for him in the hall of the luminous dead. I stand quite apart from the drama of his life before death, and shall on no account let myself be smothered by the steady, uprising swell which the controversies are bound to raise about that drama. Whatever their motives, or however inspired, these controversies can have no interest for me. I can watch dispassionately the contrasted shades of opinion tossing from pole to pole, and it makes no difference to me whether Bapuji is set down as but dead wood, which for some unaccountable reason floated down from the primordial sludge as if to choke the urge of our dynamic age, or is worshipped fervently as another Rama or Krishna in our expanding pantheon. Emotions which follow in the wake of catastrophic change plunge the human soul into the welter of chaos. I have no desire to seek the truth about Bapuji at the bottom of these turgid waters.

Nor could I for a moment dream of measuring his stature in the light of his achievements before death came and put an end to his career on earth. I have to go scrupulously by his definite comment that the total meaning of life lies in the grim fact of frustration. There can be no sense to me in recounting his deeds as if to give him a chance to plead his case at the bar which sentenced him to death by open defiance. Besides, to assess his merit or credit in the light of his deeds on this earth is really to put fresh life into the mode and technique of living which was burnt to cinders on the banks of the Yamuna. Why not let the ashes lie where they are, so that fresh life may spring up, as a matter of course, and maybe his soul, at last, will find the peace which he for fifty long years sought for mankind at large.

The conclusion, however, which his comment on history pointedly implies has nothing unwholesome or ambiguous in it. It is scrupulously precise and clear — history, whether it is of our own making or is just a pattern chosen for us has produced no results which can be called truly positive. Its long course never marked any achievement or realization, since the main trend in which it was set promised no fulfilment except that of the negative. I have no doubt there is ample evidence in human experience to confirm this conclusion, if only we seek for it.

One can with reason uphold that till today neither man nor his hostile nor friendly neighbour had the slightest chance of reaching fulfilment of any scheme they ever conceived as to the main goal of life. Instead, the total result of all efforts, human or non-human, has been clean and vivid frustration; and for man in particular, compared to the other denizens of the earth, the scale and magnitude of the universe never appeared except in the baffling shape of discipline and pain. Even what seemed sustaining and wholesome turned out sooner or later to be but a make-believe or device, the aim of which was to cast a spell over the lurid scene or to put uncanny urge into the jaded spirit of man, so that he could continue the desperate fight. Whether we move in the realm of faith or speculate boldly to unravel the truth, or build like giants what we call States to guard our interests, no God or Truth has stood firm or stable; nor has there been Art on which to place beauty as if on a throne, or State by which to drive from our doors the eternal wolves. There have been often enough great upheavals as we moved from sphere to sphere; paeans of joy and glory went up from the human hearth side by side with the piercing, heartrending cries. But sooner or later both the quick and slow upheavals, however they moved us, ended in despair. History produced no results that were positive; its keynote was negation, pure and simple.

And it is this poignant truth about history that was testified to by the manner in which Gandhi came to lose his life at the hands of violence. Whatever his ideas about life, or the efforts to realize those ideas, death gave him most unerringly the sense of complete frustration. No ideal, whether his own as a Hindu or that of his opponent, the European, could have survived for him after his death. Nor could any of the techniques fare better, and certainly it was not as a detached spirit that he left his earthly haunts as did so many of his forbears. His deepest conviction at the moment of death was that neither of the two values or techniques was capable of positive fulfilment.

I do not see how one can possibly help making this unusual claim on behalf of Bapuji; nor is it possible for me to interpret his comment on any other hypothesis. If I have to accept the comments as his own, and I do believe that somehow or other they came from him, the interpretation of them stands.

And yet one may, if necessary, support even this unusual claim about history with at least some evidence. It should not be difficult to prove that between them the life and death of Gandhi clearly marked a dual frustration of values.

There can be no doubt that his life, judged by what it actually achieved, was after all an achievement in frustrating a value, and one that was opposed to his own. It was by no means a realization of a value.

Nobody, for instance, questions the claim that it was he more than anybody else in India, who liberated his countrymen from bondage and made India independent and free. It is common knowledge that it was Gandhi who brought back the call of our ancestry from the depths into which it had fallen, and flooded the countryside with it. Here is the main clue to the liberation.

But what did this long-awaited liberation after all mean? Was it by any chance another name for the realization of the value or ideal for which he, under the command of his ancestry, openly stood? Did it knit together the human race in one close fellowship of love and unity and abolish once and for ever warfare from the society of man?

It would be unjust and unfair to his memory if we forgot that he died at the hands of violence, brokenhearted. Besides, not even our liberated ancient land is yet free from conflicts, far less the wider and more distant horizon in which the dark clouds seem to be gathering again for the next stage of warfare. On no account can the liberation of India be taken as the realization of the value or ideal which our ancestors never ceased to preach, and with which our Bapuji was perfectly at one. It meant only the removal from the spirit of our ancestry of bondage which the modern age of Europe imposed on it, and which the natural ally of the Englishman in India thoughtlessly prolonged. Here was an altogether negative process which only dispelled the fog which had settled on our land ever since the Englishman, the individualist from Europe, perhaps by some deep urge of his own conscience, occupied that land. It literally compelled the Englishman to leave India, and the Moslem Leaguer to retire to the outskirts of our ancestral land. And as, by that supreme act of frustrating the opponents of our heritage, the long night of foreign rule came to an end, the chances arose to bring back the "Moral State" and make the youth once again go back to the ethics of Vedanta and Buddha, Krishna and Rama.

But can anybody claim that in all these indispensable changes in our social existence there was evidence of a clear realization of our main ideal or value? Did not the disappearance of British rule from India after two long centuries mark only the frustration of the Englishman's attempt to establish his own value, so strange to our own in the ancient land of India? What else is the meaning of his almost miraculous hasty retreat from India? And how again, can one interpret even the retreat of the Mohammadan to the mountain fastnesses except as a miserable failure to revive the dream of Aurangzeb which irrevocably set in the decline of the Mogul rule?

It is impossible to miss the steady frustration during the last fifty years of the whole-hearted English attempt to make India part and parcel of her political scheme, and to gather her vast society into the folds of the European. And it is only natural that today — except for a very small minority who are at a loss between the fresh call of their ancestry and the loyalty bred in them to a secular goal — there should be no group of Indians who swear by the European faith. And even if the new State in India takes on, as if under duress, a form which to all appearances looks like a modern State, it will not stay long in its borrowed plumes. Perhaps even the new *elite* of Europe may come forward to help in the renewal of the Moral State as an essential for the establishment of world peace. And the Muhammadan question will solve itself as fast as it arose as the Indian State reverts to its indigenous form, a form which, between them, the Hindu and Muhammadan have preserved for long centuries with punctilious care.

There can be no question about the precise nature of the achievement of Gandhi during the years he spent on this earth. If it was an achievement of no mean proportion, it did not by any chance consist in the realization of a value. What was achieved for certain was the frustration of a value. By it the Englishman was finally frustrated in his attempt over two long centuries to establish in the ancient land of India a cult of individualism, and the class society which is germane to it. As the Brahmo Samaj and Ramakrishna Mission in Bengal in the early part of British rule met the challenge of the Christian missions Gandhi neutralized the English efforts to replace the group scheme of Indian society by its opposite model, the capitalist State. Here was an achievement in our history on a scale unparalleled and unheard of; it brought back the pure air of independence which had ceased to blow for many a long century.

But once it has begun to blow again, it may not cease until it has blown over all lands, even those far away across the distant seas. It is only gradually as time goes on that the full significance of our Bapuji will appear. In any case, his main object was to bring peace and unity to the human home, so that the liberation of his beloved India was but a step in the long process of redeeming human rights. As a Hindu he was out to liberate all men in all lands from bondage to individualism. There was nothing sectarian or even national in his outlook on life. What he, with his whole heart, wanted was the establishment of the Moral State in place of the legal, to make persuasion the technique and mode of settling differences rather than force and violence, in all lands and under all climes.

It is quite another story whether the Moral State will not only duly return to its native soil, the continent of India, but also with firm intent march across the wide seas to supersede all the legal states of the world. There is at least nothing incalculable or prohibitive in such a consummation if we go by the periodic changes which occur in history. If the Legal State could conscientiously march across the seas to the mainlands of Asia, it stands to reason that the Moral State would equally conscientiously repeat the process, though in the reverse way. There is at least nothing in the law which history has evolved to forbid such an adjustment of rights. At any rate, Gandhi, like all men of faith, did believe that it was the Legal State that was the real evil on earth; and if he fully succeeded in uprooting the legal state which the English established in India, he might well have believed that the whole of Europe would be converted to his creed. The certain fact remains that he did frustrate the Englishman in India and paved the way for the establishment of the Moral State in his beloved country. His life bore full evidence for achieving frustration of a value, and there was no sign in it of any realization.

II

The Long Night of History

Have we then to conclude that there was no realization of values to the credit of our Bapuji during the time he spent on earth, or is it open to us still to hope that what he could not achieve by his deeds was actually realized by the manner in which he died?

The answer is in the negative. Death is not a phenomenon which can be supposed either to create or to realize any value, if we distinguish it from life. It marks just the painful interlude when a value either disappears for good or goes into abeyance. Its peculiar nature is to produce a vacuum in the place of some presence — a condition which gives one the chance of at least referring to what is called the absent or the past. That a value should be realized in the course of death while it is literally coming to pass is more than human mind can think, although death is by no means what the philosopher calls "the negative", in which nothing is or happens. It is immaterial whether the human being loses his life at the hands of fellow human beings, or dies a so-called natural death at the hands of unknown creatures or things. There can be no record of achievement in death, as there can be of life, it can only be referred to as we refer to what the philosophers call "pure experience". Death is an enigma, but a fact.

Could the death of our Bapuji then have provided for a realization of value which his life of last fifty long years did not provide? Did the society of man come to be knit together in the fellowship of love and unity as death overtook him in the shape of violence? Did his death and the unity in the human family come together?

There are many leading minds in India today who seriously hold that he became truly immortal as death came to him unbidden and unsought; it was not really death as we know it, but a blessing, the highest that history holds on record. Gandhi is not dead, but lives on as at least some of our mythical figures do. And the people who loved him and held him as a god on earth simply do not believe that he has left them at the mercy of fate. Millions again are intent on doing hard penance if only to safeguard his presence in their lives and guarantee the blessings that derive from it. Still, bursts of lamentations rent the sky as the body of our Bapuji was given over to the flames, and not even a sceptic would dispose of them as myth. But in the depth of this grief which the whole continent poured out there was a faith that Bapuji cannot die. It was the human way, by a long tradition of adoring the true and pure who never can leave mankind till all suffering has ceased.

But is Bapuji really alive today as he certainly was only the other day, when the bullet struck him dead? Did he listen to our heartrending cry as we gave him over to the flames? Was he moved by our deep humility and faith in the presence of his death?

Human mind as a matter of long habit normally inclines to the faith that life is continuous and unbroken, and one of the chief marks of our kinship with all men and women appears in this faith. As if by an axiom, we all came to this earth together and shall leave it if necessary exactly as we came. Perhaps the home which men built with toil is also another evidence of this same old faith; the solidarity of man is attested by it, and neither kinship nor solidarity is possible if death is allowed ruthlessly to break the bonds. Man therefore never dies, since the loss of one man may spell disaster for the whole species, and so runs the faith.

But the grim fact remains that Bapuji did die, and he died at the hands of violence, completely broken-hearted. And if the surge of grief rose like the sea as death came like a bolt from the blue heavens, it did not make any impression on him; it could not, since he was simply no longer there to receive it. There was unmistakably a barrier between him as he died and the loud lamentations that followed in a trail to his death. In an instant, sooner than one could think, all relationship between him and the world he had known was gone. It should be impossible to miss this truth about death at this stage of the universe. Something at least does go out of existence at death, and the attempt to soften the severity of that loss by classifying death under the category of change is not even wise. We cannot forget that by his death we have lost our Bapuji for good, and that in a sense that matters. The gift of his death was sorrow and not joy, the hardest one can meet. It left us with a vacuum which cannot be filled, and if other experiences begin to flow in time to assuage our grief, that one blind spot, his death, will never be lit up again. Still, curiously enough, even death as a phenomenon occurs; it is not "nothing" in which nothing happens, and so it truly means experience like any that life produces. Bapuji had a full share of that experience, and for him it was a pang or anguish of the soul, a sense of frustration after a life-long effort to fulfil. But nobody on this earth, not to say his fellow men and women, had a share in it. It was self-absorbed like a cup full to the brim which he alone could drink. Our sorrow was of another brew, he had no taste of it. We know for certain that death took him; we know nothing else.

Should we still look for a realization of value in his death if we did not find it in the whole of his life? Did his death embody a fulfilment of unity and love which his life certainly did not? Did our Bapuji feel as the bullet struck him that the militant Hindu, or Muhammad Ali Jinnah, or Winston Churchill came to be united to him, and peace prevailed on earth?

We are already in the advanced years of the modern age; we have at least to be precise in our thought and rational in our expectations. It is late in the day, and may at any moment be too late for the preservation of the species, if we still perpetuate our pious hopes and seek relief in mere emotions. We may do penance in as rigorous a form as we please, but what difference will penance make to death, which, without any conscience, took Bapuji away? Could we ever eliminate that moment of death from its place in history once it had found it? Could we undo the anguish of frustration which that moment meant for him? If penance leads to blessings from the gods, do we not collect them for or from those who are living and not dead? Can they by any chance unmake the fact of death, as if Bapuji was never done to death, or felt in death the doom that crashed over his head?

These are by no means enigmatic issues; nor is it wise for us in the twentieth century, after experiments for 5,000 years, to go back to the "eternal verities" for consolation and peace. We might easily do injury to the memory of our Bapuji whom we love, if we sought assurance in the thought that the eternal verities for which he stood would gather him back to the home of eternal peace. Nobody had more confidence and trust in divine guidance than Gandhi. "God or the spirit of truth above and the moral law within" was his motto of life. Even in acute moments of doubt and despair he did not swerve by an inch from it. But how did the "verities" stand when a life-long experiment on no other basis than on what they themselves indicated most miserably failed? Where was their authority then, not to say the ground of their claim to the loyalty and devotion of the creatures on earth?

It need not be a sacrilege to urge that the "verities" never once came out of their residence in the eternal realm of divinity. It seems inscrutable that the creatures of the earth should have to skim the mud for sheer self-preservation, and, as if that were not severe enough that they should have to give up their lives at the hands of violence even though they fulfilled to the letter all the commandments laid down for them.

And yet, there may be a meaning in the fact that such an apparent travesty of justice and love is allowed to happen in the universe. God or the Eternal Verities may well be there for all we know; but it is not the time to discover where exactly they dwell: it may well be that we have hitherto chosen a path to find their residence which could not possibly lead to it. Yet again, why this mistake should have been made may be our own concern and not that of the God in the heavens or the Verities which are credited with eternal life. If Bapuji died at the hands of violence it was for Bapuji and his fellowmen to appreciate the significance of that failure, and not to run up to the heavens that are not there to demand an explanation. It is patent that no demon would or could have given a worse deal than the God of history or the Verities have given us if we go by values and ideals we have hitherto cherished. It is no longer possible for us to preach and practise those values after Bapuji's death. There is no guarantee left in them for consolidating peace or uprooting the challenge to love. If death distilled the anguish of the human soul so carefully laid in the womb of the universe and offered it as an absolution to our Bapuji for eternal peace, nothing is left to us but a mockery of those ideals. It is not open to us to preach love and peace if the final effort in human history to establish them brought only misery and shame which like the everbounding tongues of flame touched the roof of the earth.

There was no realization of value in Bapuji's death; there was only frustration of value, and this time it was the value or ideal which he cherished which failed. As he frustrated the Englishman and the Muhammadan by his fifty years of hard and strenuous work to liberate his beloved land, so they frustrated him in his over-reaching attempt to establish peace and love in the human home. His life and death between them form the only instance in human history for dual frustration, and this bears clear evidence to the conclusion as to the implication of his comments on history. History produced only negative results, there has been no realization of any positive value yet.

III

An Experiment with Tradition

But does this conclusion stand without any precedent in the history of the human race? Did no other figure in the long human tradition come to the same conclusion about the history they were familiar with in their time? Can this conclusion, again, be taken as only a repetition of the sceptical view, one which stood for complete inaction on the part of mankind on the ground that Reality was not, or in its more modest form, that ideals or values were nothing but myths or legends which only bemused the gods?

Both issues are equally significant and real, they deserve to be analysed with great precision and care. It is, however, only in the analysis of the latter that the specific message of our Bapuji as to the age that is imminent will be found. Besides, my own estimate of our Bapuji will wholly rest on that message and not on anything else that stands to his credit. Personally, it is not possible that I should not draw a line between his life which embodied his deeds and him as he appeared after his death to make me familiar with his latest thoughts. Here was a transition in the career of our Bapuji, however mysterious, and the point I am making is that the whole of his life was but an experiment with tradition with confidence and wisdom proportionate to the age in which he lived. I do not certainly judge him in terms of what he said or did in his life as everybody else almost necessarily does; to me all his sayings and deeds were but grist to the mill of his experiments, clean hypotheses that were put to the test of verification. Both when he stood firm in conviction, or wavered in doubt or even despair, he was equally in the hands of investigation or proof. There was not any marked evidence in his career for a stand for absolutism or of a dogmatic vigour in his spirit which takes no account of the challenge from the other side. His lot was cast, as it were, on the mud floor of our social home, the milieu where millions live and die, so that he could assure them and himself whether the ideal of love was true. Not even for a moment was there a desire in him to seek detachment from fellow human beings. In a very real sense the State was his sole concern and the whole of his life was one continuous effort to make it a home for harmony and peace; verily, it is that effort that flamed continuously as the one experiment of his life. It would be unfair to his memory if we judge of his life by anything fixed as a standard. The truth is that his life was nothing but a search for a standard as if he were never quite sure of any.

An adequate review of history, however, is not possible for a variety of reasons. I can only select a few outstanding cases and those that I shall deal with stand in the records of the sixth century BCE and the first century CE.

If I take the case of Gautama the Buddha who lived in the sixth century BCE, his comment on history may almost appear as a parallel to that of Gandhi after his death. Even if it is disputed that he ever made any such comment — there are claims that he did make such comments — his main contention that life up to his time had been one long tale of suffering from birth to death was sufficient evidence that history produced nothing but negative results. He was fully aware of the systematic efforts that had been made in the long past before his age, in both the speculative and practical fields to produce positive results. Whether one considers the Vedic sacrifices or the ascetic practices or the metaphysical speculations or the life of man and woman in society governed by the State, the achievements of all these varied efforts, according to the Buddha, were absolutely nil. And it would make no difference to his charge against all these profound and strenuous attempts to make life yield positive results even if the ideals happened to be tested in the course of long centuries.

And it is too late in the day to argue that the results of these efforts were positive and not negative, even though they were frankly and fully nothing but "suffering" pure and simple. Such a contention will leave no room for the distinction that is drawn between the positive and the negative, or suffering and happiness. Nor will it preserve even a semblance to conflict by its hidden implication that it breaks out invariably between right and right or good and good. The claim to reduce not only the conflicts between opposites but also variety and multiplicity to a monistic identity is difficult to follow, for the simple reason that if the opposites or the multiple ever arose in human experience, they could not possibly be transmuted into harmony and simplicity. What is conceivable is that they may in course of time disappear altogether and in their places the harmonious and the simple may appear. But that consummation must be an actual fact before the opposites or the multiple could be denied as the only fact in existence. It is inconceivable that the multiple and simple or the harmonious and the conflicting should be existing side by side.

We can only conclude that history, according to the Buddha, up to the sixth century BCE was nothing if not negative in its achievement. It literally produced negative results, since life in the sixth century BCE, as before, however far back one might go, was one stretch of unqualified suffering.

Equally clear is the nature of the claim about history which might be legitimately attributed to Jesus in the first century CE, provided we accept the Christian gospel of the divinity of Christ, and view Jesus in the light which was thrown on his personality by the claim that truth came into this world with his appearance on earth. If there was no truth in the world in spite of the fact that the world was there, there was either falsehood or illusion, which certainly was not truth. The results, therefore, which were expected to be produced by an effort, the keynote of which was either illusion or falsehood, could not be positive. And the same conclusion follows from the Christian gospel of the Divinity of Christ. If there was no Divinity in the world before Jesus appeared on earth in Bethlehem, there was either Satan or some pale facsimile of Satan without his alleged malice. The results in such a world would not certainly be positive, since neither truth nor love would have a share in their derivation. It is another story whether Jesus should be judged altogether in the light of the Christian doctrine of Divinity of Christ or the identification of truth with his personality. I am not discussing what actually Jesus himself did hold as to the claims of history; that is not an issue which is either relevant to my thesis about history or falls within the reach of my scholastic competence. One wishes certainly one could be assured about Jesus as one is assured about the Buddha, but since both the Christian doctrine about Divinity and the appearance of truth with the advent of Jesus on the dark horizon of the world have been firmly held for centuries, there is no reason why I should not claim on behalf of Jesus that perhaps he too held the same view about history as the Buddha and Gandhi did.

And it makes no difference even if I have to note that history to Jesus meant a span of time which was at least 600 years longer than that of Buddha. What Buddha himself would have said about the additional 600 years after his death if he had a chance of commenting on them as Jesus is supposed to have done it is futile to ask. But it may be pointed out that Gandhi on 30 January 1948, two thousand six hundred years after Buddha died, made the same comment on history as Jesus did on the 600 years after Buddha. In any case, if we take the Buddha, Jesus and Gandhi, as three outstanding landmarks in human history, we find that the claim to positive realization in any period of history is completely neutralized. The three periods comprising — the millennia from the beginning, however nebulous in its formation, till the sixth century BCE; the 600 years from the sixth century BCE to the first century CE; and the 2,000 years from the first century CE to the twentieth century, are written off by the three figures in succession as devoid of any fulfilment but altogether replete with negative results.

The question, however, arises whether Buddha, Jesus and Gandhi meant by the phrase "negative results" exactly the same thing. No doubt "negative results" according to them all meant results which followed from the frustration of a value, as distinguished from its realization. The Buddha did mean that the ideals and values of life were completely frustrated till the sixth century BCE. The evidence for that claim consisted in the fact that life to him was nothing but suffering and suffering, it was taken for granted, could not be accepted as a sign of the fulfilment or realization of value. It was peace or harmony instead that was considered to be a sign of fulfilment.

Equally clear it is that history was frustration and not realization up to the first century CE, since, according to Jesus, it was falsehood and sin and not truth or virtue that marked the career of the world till the first century CE. Man was born in sin and the world was subject to the rule and authority of Satan till the Christian era began. So there was in the world nothing but frustration; there could not be anything else since there was no truth or divinity to guide human life or the world.

And nothing could be more evident than that Gandhi frankly meant by "negative results", frustration of values. In fact, in him, as we have already pointed out, there was dual frustration.

But can it be held that they all meant by frustration of values complete disappearance of the values or ideals as they have been known in history? Did either the Buddha or Jesus hold or imply that all conceivable values were frustrated or done to death as Gandhi after his death literally did?

This is a very difficult and complicated issue. It is one thing to quote opinions and adduce evidences to show that the Buddha and Jesus both held that history up to their time produced no fulfilment, a different thing to claim that their views admitted only of one interpretation. In any case, we have to note the fact that both of them came to map out a future for the human race in which they were fully convinced that the negative results of the past would be completely replaced by the positive. If they took a negative view of the past, they did not equally suspect the future age of the universe. They were fully convinced, on the contrary, that one could escape frustration altogether, provided that the mode and manner of living was radically changed. The Buddha was certain that the eightfold path would lead to the complete removal of suffering from human life, while the Sermon on the Mount or the doctrine of love was for Jesus a panacea for all evil.

If, however, their ideal or technique for the future was but a reformulation of an old ideal or technique, it would be difficult to take their claim about "negative results" as absolute. If the stand for the individual in the group scheme of life and the final achievement of peace in *nirvana* was a repudiation of the scheme for hierarchy and absorption in the mystical entity, it could by no means be unhistorical. It could not be, since in the nature of things, history was not the stage which could dramatize only the one or the other view — I mean the mystical and hierarchical or the humanistic and equalitarian. The universe or human history, was necessarily conceived in a dichotomy, the constituents of which were either mysticism and humanism, or unity and freedom.

There was no period in which both of them in some sense or other were not present, and it was inevitable that either the one or the other view would always prevail unless there were deadlock or confusion. The Buddha must be supposed to have reformulated the humanistic and equalitarian view of the group scheme while Jesus simply introduced the mystical and hierarchical view into the individualistic scheme. There was nothing radical in their position and claim in the sense that they were creating altogether new values for human existence. They were, on the contrary, as true to the spirit and technique of history as their opponents were, and if they differed considerably from one another, the reason was that between them, they were holding two incompatible ideals and techniques.

One has to draw the conclusion, therefore, that neither the Buddha nor Jesus could have meant by their dictum about the negative results of history something really absolute. Theirs was not a case of complete and wholesale repudiation of history as such. If still it was a repudiation, its direct effect bore on the humanistic and mystical views of history separately, and not on both of them at the same time. And perhaps, while they reformulated the old historical views, they implied equally a repudiation of the forms in which they had prevailed in the past. The Buddha's stand for humanism of the group scheme was by no means a repetition of the old stand for the same creed, exactly as Jesus cannot be supposed to have simply transported Hindu mysticism into the individualist scheme of the Western peoples. In some sense, therefore, it may still be held that history up to the time when they taught produced negative results.

But can it be held that Gandhi was only another landmark in the same process of partial negation like Buddha and Jesus? Did he too mean by negative results only a negation of one of the ideals, however complete, and a rejection of the dead form of the other?

The answer to me is not in the affirmative; the negative in Gandhi's case was, if anything, not partial but strictly absolute. In so far as between his life and death they were responsible for nothing less than frustration of both the values no phase or portion of tradition survived as operative factors after Gandhi. The whole of history as a significant phenomenon went into the melting pot. So that today there is absolutely no ideal or value left for us on which to work, if we mean to be serious and precise.

One still may add that our future, at any rate, did not suffer at the hands of this meteoric phenomenon — I mean the life and death of Gandhi — in the same way as the whole of our recorded past did. It is even permitted to hope that the elimination of the "past", as totally effete and negative, has for the first time made the real future possible. In any case, we shall soon have the chance to visualize that possibility. But it was complete frustration of our historic tradition that was brought about by Gandhi's life and death — a phenomenon which never appeared in human history. At any rate, none of them — I mean the Buddha, Socrates and Jesus, to mention only the nearest parallels to Gandhi — even approximated to the level of negation which Gandhi frankly demonstrated.

Literally, the whole epoch which we call human civilization and whose span is counted as at least 6,000 years came to a close as the bullets from his opponent finished the earthly career of Gandhi. There was no longer any foundation left to the incessant struggle between individualism and universalism which constituted the core of human civilization. As if after long and repeated cycles the primal demands of the human heart — unity and freedom — which met and fought like giants and invariably left the field in complete confusion, suddenly decided not to repeat the cycle of fighting: or to vary the metaphor, the planets which with bursting inward flames set their movements at the very dawn of creation suddenly vanished into a cavern of darkness if only to reappear as a steadily towering monolith pointing to the star in one unbroken line.

This is by no means a markedly modest claim. I have no reason, however, to moderate it or to append an apology to soften its vigour.

I am fully convinced that Gandhi's deliberate onslaught on the creed of individualism as it has been in operation during the last two or three centuries gave it a mortal blow. It is not possible that it should again revive, so that Asia, or more properly that part of the world which has been the home of group civilization within known times, will not have to submit again to the will or authority of the European. There will be instead an opportunity for the Asian not only to recover steadily from the effects of the long European occupation but to rebuild his own economy by a technique which he had to abandon under pressure from the European. It is this possibility which marks the true achievement of Gandhiji. And certainly it meant no offence to the European creed; it had in view only freedom and independence for the group civilization and not hostility to the individualistic scheme. If, however, by sinister chance, the European still cherishes the dream of re-entering Asia, and this time with the sheer dead weight of scientific and industrial might, that will be a sure sign that the group scheme or the Moral State, will inevitably cross the seas and overwhelm the whole of the European home.

Once the spirit of individualism has been broken on the mainland of Asia, it cannot be rejuvenated on the basis of its material backbone, however solid. A civilization lives in and for the ideal which it embodies; the technique that works out that ideal follows the line as it is laid down by that ideal. If the ideal of a civilization suffers demise at the hands of its antagonist, its technique will not escape the doom or survive as mere technique. My claim is that the spirit or ideal of individualism as it prevailed in the last two centuries all over the world was broken in twain by Gandhiji, and this historic demise was illustrated by what looked like the self-immolation in India of the British Rule. The funeral pyre on which the pride of the British individualist was burnt antedated only by a year the pyre which burnt to cinders the Doctrine of Love. One almost feels that the air is still much too thick with the smoke from the two historic pyres. It would be more than a miracle if the ideals or values that were burnt in them were resurrected; at any rate, neither the spirit of Islam, lying in peaceful sleep now for centuries, nor the elan of the neo-European who dreams in terms of technique will achieve that miracle. The rhythm of history will stop that miracle if nothing else will. Either the "bomb" will not burst or it will, like a boomerang, come back to the European. Whatever attempts can be made now to revive the dead spirit of individualism whether by machination or deliberate perversion of truth or by an organized "hooliganism", they will only hasten the complete collapse of individualism. Such a calamity is too heavy a price for the human species to pay, so I take it there will be no occasion to pay it.

There can be no sense in restaging individualism in the name of freedom and peace, and what is equally true, there is even less reason for preaching universalism, as if that were the only creed that God in the heavens formulated for the human race. There is, at least, no indication of such a message in the manner in which Gandhi took leave of his human frame. His death was the last milestone in the long trek in pursuit of unity and love. This long journey of centuries finally came to an end as Gandhiji breathed his last, and it is not open to any of us to go on that fateful journey again. If still we make a fresh attempt to realize love and unity, in spite of the warning in that historic death, it will be like tracing one's steps in the vacuum or empty air. The discipline set by human conscience or cosmic urge in the shape of pursuit of love and unity as opposed to freedom and independence reached its limit when fifty years' continuous attempt to realize it in the heart of the twentieth century met its doom at the hands of violence.

If, still, it is not possible that we should give up altogether our quest of freedom and love, we have at least to review or reformulate them. We cannot possibly re-stage the drama of love and unity without a radical change both in their form and outline, exactly as we cannot repeat our quest of freedom in the sense and form in which we have hitherto held it. The fact is that a completely fresh formulation of our ideals and technique has fallen due, a vision of which was enshrined in Gandhi's life and death. If it brought to a close the long experiment of history which we call civilization, it also foreshadowed the sure beginning of a new epoch. At least our race has been at the parting of the ways ever since the moment in which the death of Gandhiji occurred; we are called upon by it to ring out the old, which gave us no breathing space in the midst of continuous struggle but only a taste of discipline proportionate to it, and ring in the new which promises at least a cessation of warfare and a regulation of life all round. And what this fresh and new life in human society can mean it will be easy to visualize as we discuss the issue of scepticism in connection with Gandhi's conclusion about history.

IV

Mystics, Humanists and Sceptics

It might be necessary, however, to discuss an outstanding claim in our ancestral history before we launch out on our investigation whether Gandhiji did or did not imply the sceptical conclusion by his stand for dual frustration as the total achievement of history. That claim is that if in the long course of our civilization every school of thought and practice steadily appeared, not excluding the non-theistic, humanistic and sceptical, there had been a persistent background of mysticism against which all negative views reacted.

And it is here, according to this robust claim, that the very core of our ancestry lies. No other single tradition in our long history can compare with it as truly representative of the Hindu mind. Besides, here is something distinctly positive which, like the shore firmly lying against the sea, never yielded to the incessant lapping of the waves of criticism.

As a matter of fact, no civilization can be supposed to have evolved just the bare negative view. If the sceptic appeared duly in the course of all types of civilization, his unfailing appearance implied that there had already been the dogmatic schools, a clash between which alone could lead to scepticism. The bare, absolute negative, except in the speculation of the human mind, never could or did constitute the universe. The society of men could not have survived in the grip of just the bare negative faith, or as an epitome or embodiment of the belief that nothing is and no value is real or achievable. And if, further, all instances of society sooner or later ended necessarily in confusion or scepticism, which made of the negative the supreme value or the chief evidence for reality, they did not originate as sheer masterpieces of confusion.

The mystical tradition in our civilization which marked the inception of it, never disappeared from its horizon even in the heyday of rampant scepticism. Since the social scheme which gave birth to it was the group scheme, that scheme had punctiliously to make room for it in its large, unwieldy proportion. If, indeed, even the fetish worshipper could be accommodated in that vast, generous bosom known as the caste society, it is inconceivable that the Vedantist should have missed a place by the side of the sceptic. Besides, the scepticism of the group scheme did not emulate the credal extreme of its anti-type, the individualist. No conceivable view or practice was ruled out in the group scheme except only that which was espoused by the creed of the individualist. Not even the group scheme could make room for its contrary or for the contradictory.

But does it follow from its sheer persistence in our long history that mysticism must be supposed to have escaped the negative result? Can the mere survival of a faith serve as an evidence for the success or realization of that faith?

No doubt it is not an evidence for its demise or abeyance. On the contrary, the fact is that the doctrine of love and unity, whatever the reasons, never went out of Hindu life; it was fully operative even up to the moment when Gandhi breathed his last. And both lay and sophisticated opinion claim today that even his death did not make any difference to mysticism. In fact, the ascetic world which took a not very generous view of Gandhiji would laugh at the suggestion that Gandhiji's death marked the end of mysticism. There are many minds, again, in India and outside India who frankly cherish the thought that if mysticism had a chance to fulfil its mission in the modern age, that chance arose most assuredly as soon as violence took the life of Gandhiji. It is openly repeated that what his life could not achieve by deeds, was literally achieved by his death, which by all historical canons, did not embody any action but instead complete inaction or absolute quiet.

Human mind is a variegated pattern into which, as time went on, many a strand was woven; it is not possible that it should or must always think or act on the basis of a uniform standard or value. Nor is it a fact that it ever solemnly abjured the right to fall into contradiction simply because it overvalued consistency at times. The only permanence that human mind most unquestionably claimed was the bare profession of one cardinal right. It religiously held that it would not commit suicide either in thought or practice; it was convinced that as a being, eternally real, it was imperative for it that it must go by the well-known law which arranged the positive and the negative in fixed relationship. One can be, in other words, both rational and consistent or irrational and inconsistent but one cannot break the law of contradiction whether in thought or action — one cannot be rational and irrational at the same time.

But could we argue from this ultimate situation that the mystic solved the problem of life if only because we have to hold that he is today perhaps as fully alive as he has ever been?

There are many minds, at least, in India who hold the affirmative view, of whom some of the most authoritative openly base their contention on verified results rather than on strictly logical grounds. It is not exactly the theory of mysticism, however persistent, but the strictly mystical way of life that is adduced by these minds as the main source of their evidence. They anxiously refer to the actual lives which the mystics lived, and those not merely of the great towering figures well known in history, but also of the devoted rank and file. Besides, the claim is made on the definite ground that those who led the mystic way of life reached at the end of their long, ascetic practices not only a strong and clean sense of detachment from all life but complete and perfect control over both body and mind. They stood in the surrounding welter of life literally unruffled and in perfect peace. As if the world which ran wild either with joy or sorrow all around them suddenly became non-existent for them. And yet, somehow, they never left their fellow human beings; and the greatest of them, at any rate, chose even to forgo the right to instant salvation in the interest of those who were still destitute and in pain.

It would be ungracious to dispose of these achievements as fiction or to consider the evidences adduced on behalf of them as sheer verbiage. If ever there comes the day to watch the ascetics leaving the world in a body under pressure from their rivals, the humanists, their places will not be filled by their rotund antagonists, but by the sheer enigma of restless vacuum. Not even the universe would survive if by any chance any real harm came to the ascetic world. The mystics must be there at their posts like their antagonists, if the human species expects to sustain its right to live. It would be lunacy to assert that no light came from the faith or practices of the ascetic world. Mankind would long ago have been swallowed up by sheer overflow of the primeval mud if the light emanating from the ascetic rigour had not illumined our sky. We should be literally herding together in deathless fright, in a trackless universe, like a race of desperate cowards if the ascetic had not enlivened us by, at least, a vivid tale of a limitless world. That tale was like the light which in spite of the ever-stretching marshes makes a clearing so that the birds overhead may fly.

It would be fatal and perverse to throw out the ascetic as if he were wastage, only to bring in the insistent humanist. Most assuredly, the ascetic holds a place in our society, and the place which is his by right is also the pivot of our social home. He filled it with extreme piety and resilience; were not the blessings which human civilization gratefully collected at his hands many and varied? Could we but go back to those days when the human home, in the midst of surrounding darkness, lit up as the long, ascetic rigour exuded light which dispelled that darkness! How gratefully mankind after a breathless effort to live breathed again with faith and hope when that light spread out in the sky! These are facts of history, and such facts we treasure up as gold and call civilization.

It is a different issue, however, whether that ascetic rigour and compassion which never faltered, did for good lift the clouds which sat solidly on the brow of the human home. It would be difficult to maintain that the human race or any section of it ever became truly peaceful as the ascetic benignly wanted it to be, or that after the Mystic had spoken seeds were never sown again which could sprout with warfare. What actually happened was that the age of the mystics brought in with it an assurance and calm the like of which was never known. There came peace to the human home which made warfare impossible for a time. But this peace did not endure. Sooner or later the community went back to its previous mood in which it stood for freedom and not peace at the cost of freedom, and engaged in warfare again to consolidate freedom at the cost of unity. The Mystics gradually retreated and the whole economy which supported their claim and embodied the fruits of their efforts went underground.

History has been only a stage on which the mystic and the humanist alternately rose and fell; there was no instance in it which proved or verified the absoluteness of either claim. Each of them prevailed for a time and then it looked as if the human problem was actually solved. Curiously it is these periods of our history, periods which mark the rise of civilization, which shine like the spring blossoms after the depressing rigour of winter. We treasure them as gold and live on them as if they formed the very sap of our life. But no period in our history when either the mystic or the humanist prevailed did really shine like pure gold. There was always some dross mixed up in it. The mystic had to suppress the humanist exactly as the humanist had to destitute the mystic as the one or the other came to prevail. The glory that we call civilization was not without a shadow, and since it was of a dual type, the shadows constantly moved from one side to the other as the standard of civilization came to be raised by the mystics or the humanists in turn. And so most fatefully the captives and the slaves only changed their places — there was never a time when they disappeared from either type. They remained in all civilizations right through, either in open shame or under heavy disguises. No splendour or glory was ever without a note of anguish sounding right through its heart. Either there was a display of that anguish from the sheer excess of it or it was deliberately muffled for the sake of conscience. The truth of history is that if the mystic never became identified with the humanist, the humanist never had his integrity impaired. The worst that ever happened to them was that for a time they did not know how to defend themselves or to avoid the bitter taste of conversion to the opposite faith. There was even a moment when they respectively believed that justice was after all unity, or love only another name for freedom of spirit.

And yet all these are elementary truths which a review of any history will bear out provided we keep to its primary feature and inner significance. There is at least nothing in history to contradict them except the dogmatic views which mutually stand contradicted.

The history, however, which will illustrate and establish these truths bears on the nature of the relationship which the mystics and the humanists bore to one another throughout their historical existence — by far the most central issue in their career.

There can be no question but that they stood related instead of functioning as isolated types. It was not possible that there could be any significance in their ideals or techniques, apart from the fact that they belonged as distinct groups to a social system and had for their aim the realization of its common objective. It was in a social system that they lived and functioned. They would have been literally dead outside its ranges.

Their relationship, again, with which we are directly concerned is embodied in their activities, the aim of which was nothing if not to realize the common social goal. And it is a historical fact that these activities appeared in clear and definite conflict. The Mystics and the Humanists did not blend or harmonize in their steady efforts to achieve the common ideal but positively clashed. Most unmistakably a record of their activities in history is a record of conflicts between contraries and contradictories in the shape of mystical and humanistic values.

But what exactly are the forms which the mystical and humanistic values took as they clashed as contradictories or as contraries, which are the only forms a conflict takes? What happened to them as they lived and functioned as Mystics and Humanists in their social structures with objectives and techniques proportionate to their mystical and humanistic aims?

Broadly speaking, there were two clear stages through which the conflict passed as the Mystics and the Humanists stood to each other as contradictories, while the stage of contrariety which followed was a stage of confusion or scepticism. The two stages embodied two distinct types of activities which can be described as those of construction and destruction. It is a fact that the Mystics and the Humanists not only constructed but also destroyed social structures. They exercised by turns both the functions of destruction and construction. There were periods in human history when the mystical or the humanistic social structures arose as the result of mystical and humanistic efforts; and equally there were periods when they were resolutely pulled down by the Mystics and the Humanists themselves. These two periods alternated with one another. Every construction had its own destruction to follow it, and no destruction was due if there had not been already a construction to pull down. The history of the relationship between the Mystic and the Humanist is a history in which they built-up civilizations which were inevitably destroyed, and destroyed civilizations which had been built up with faith. Nothing survived at the end of their conflict.

To illustrate this deep, unfamiliar outline in the structure of human society it may be useful to review a phase of Indian history which saw the gradual establishment of British rule in India, a phase in which the mystical and humanistic civilizations met in deadly conflict perhaps for the last time.

As the British State proceeded to establish its absolute rule, the first essential for its success was to replace the Indian village community, the indigenous, socio-political unit of the Indian State by some improvised scheme of British landlordism and capitalism. The village community, which had catered for the Indian society for long centuries, and which was not disturbed even by a few centuries of Mohammedan rule, had to go before the British State could take its place in India where the Hindu and the Mogul had ruled.

Here in the establishment of the British State in India was involved a dual process of both destruction and construction. The process of destruction appeared in the steady and gradual disappearance of the village community, and with it the structure of civilization embodied in it, which the Indian had raised in the course of centuries. What this process was and how the Indian had nothing but grim experiences in its course since the early days of the nineteenth century are historical facts which one can easily find out from the records of British rule. Equally easy it should be to follow the process of construction, the gradual and steady establishment of some type of European individualism in the place of the group system of which the Indian village community was the main central unit.

The two processes, as they gave shape to the careers of both the Englishman and the Indian since the clash between the two civilizations began, kept quite distinct and did not coincide. The experiences which resulted from them were altogether different types. There was nothing in common between the experience of the Indian as he watched the basis of his civilization being gradually uprooted and the experience of the Englishman who felt that he was removing lumber and dead wood from the path of civilization, for instance, by pulling down the village community. Nor did the Englishman or the Indian feel exactly in the same way as they both took part in building up the structure of a new civilization on the soil on which the old indigenous culture had stood. It was a work of faith for the Englishman, who had the sense of establishing civilization in the heart of Asia; and for the Indian it was partly a work of shame and partly a work to which there was no alternative.

There can be no question that the two moments of destruction and construction and the experiences which followed from them were distinct and definite. No Indian can possibly forget what it meant to him as gradually and steadily he lost his Moral State, village economy, joint family and even the ethics on which life stood, as formulated by his long ancestry. Here was the sense of loss and destruction in which there was no sign or trace of construction. The village scheme of centuries was completely destroyed. The prevailing sense was what, in the East, one has when the sky is covered from end to end with locusts. Everything was going down — it had to, before the process of construction could begin.

Nor can it be doubted that the conditions changed considerably as the period of construction set in. Everywhere there was a feeling of security and an expectation of prosperous days. Even enthusiasm for the change, and advocacy of its blessings, appeared in the educated elite and in those who helped in establishing the British State and making the British trade prosper. Nobody seemed to remember, for instance, the grim history of the weavers of Dacca muslins. It was even forgotten that there was such a thing as Village Community or such figures as the Indian architects and craftsmen, or Indian economy, or the continuous flow of fairs and festivals in which people from all parts foregathered.

The general sense which pervaded the atmosphere was one of security, peace and order, with expectations about the future. If the Englishman wholeheartedly sponsored this stage at times with an exaltation of spirit, the Indian was by no means slow in thankfully assimilating the life which was offered to him, or in giving it every possible chance to germinate on the Indian soil.

It is another story whether that life did or could germinate in the manner in which the Englishman wanted. And already the stage is being set rapidly for reversal of the process or way of living which the British introduced. Soon there will be complete elimination of all British construction and the re-establishment of the indigenous system in its place, whether the Englishman and the educated Indian like it or not. There is really no alternative to it — unless it be that of realizing Bapuji's dream, a new State altogether different from the Legal and the Moral. In any case, the phase of Indian history that we have just analysed is a clear case embodying the nature of the relationship between the Mystic and the Humanist.

The conclusion to be drawn from these two periods of construction and destruction is that there has been no fulfilment of value, whether mystical or humanistic; but only a frustration of both. What the one constructed, the other pulled down; and neither of them had anything to show in the end, except the sense of temporary freedom from bondage and destitution. Could anybody call this fluctuating process of rise and fall by the name of achievement and peace?

Yet, by the same cosmic arrangement, there were two distinct features in this constant change in fortune and misfortune which looked like an oasis in the sliding sands of the desert; and these were first, that faith and expectation never disappeared and second, that suffering or instability of fortune did not cut into the provision of justice in the historic drama. As if the spirit of the universe saw to it that neither the Mystic nor the Humanist had his own way all the time. If they had literally to walk through fire half the time in their career, it was a walk which both necessarily had to face.

V

Asceticism contra Freedom

But could the Mystic be anywhere near solving the problem of life if what we have just described as the main drama of life be true? Could the Mystic have reached salvation if mysticism or the mystical history of the human race had to suffer defeat periodically at the hands of its rival, humanism? Is it conceivable that one could dissociate the Mystic from either the mystical tradition of the human race or the social milieu in which alone the mystical experiment could be made?

This is the most important issue from the point of view of the historian, for whom no individual, whether he is a Mystic or a Humanist, counts except as a member of human society.

The strictly isolated individual who has no communion with his fellow beings and whose life may be cast in another communion, whether with Divine Presence or semi-divine spirits, is literally non-existent for the historian. Such an individual exists, if at all, only for himself, completely out of touch with man, woman or animal. He is not even an enigma for the human race and does not bring any blessings to them, as he is by definition in pursuit of Divine grace in as exclusive a form as possible. It is futile to ask whether he meets God in dreams or visions or in some rarified atmosphere of the universe. What happens between him and his God is entirely his own concern although it may sound hard to say so. The historian has no occasion to deal with such men or events and, for lay minds, the isolated individual, whatever his pedigree, is not even a myth, not to say a blessing. It is the peak of fantasy to forget one's roots either in the universe or the social scheme in which man was born and bred.

If the individual, then, with whom we have to deal has to be a member of the human community, there can be no escape for him from the rigid laws to which that community is necessarily subject. He has to be either a Mystic or a Humanist, unless he lapses into compromise; and so he is bound to go through the two periods of construction and destruction which history laid down for both mysticism and humanism. As an individual, he cannot expect under any circumstances to solve the problem of life, since neither mysticism nor humanism has solved it.

This conclusion sounds like hard saying. It cuts straight into the claim that individuals can reach salvation apart from the community in which they were born, and which made it possible for them to profess mysticism. There is indeed no hesitation in such a conclusion to repudiate the suggestion that the individual has a place outside the community or his relationship with fellow individuals. It firmly holds to the view that the individual cannot but be a being or an entity who or which must be one among many. There is no alternative to it. Technically, the notion of individuality is meaningless apart from the notion of relationship, and it is a basic fact that the world in which the individual lives is a multiple world and not monistic. So that the fortune or misfortune which is bound up with the career of the individual happens to him in that world and that world alone. Unmistakably, no individual can possibly escape the obligations which the multiple world lays down. And so salvation for the individual can only mean salvation for the community at large, whatever that might mean. If, still, one can conceive of Divinity outside the realm of the multiple universe, such a prospect need not cut into the claim of individuality or multiplicity.

Perhaps we have not seen yet the full significance or worth of the universe we belong to or of Divinity, our distant goal.

If the life of the individual then is bound up with the life of the community, it follows that no individual can expect either release from bondage or fulfilment of his objective except in relationship to every other individual. This is the strict, logical conclusion. If the factors which determine the course of the multiple universe are primarily individuality and relationship, it is difficult to see how this universal patrimony could admit of a distribution which brings inequality and injustice in its train. And conceivably there is no third factor to introduce a maladjustment. There could be nothing to neutralize the keynote of multiplicity as the ruling principle of all existence — justice and equality. Even if conflict were ordained as part or portion of the lot which was cast for the individual, there was nothing in such a provision to cut into the claims of justice and equality. If the individual could not possibly detach himself from the community, he was subject to no indignity or inequality. Whether he prevailed or went down within the range of that community, he did so exactly as his fellow individuals did according to the strict rule of justice and equality. The two processes of construction and destruction worked evenly in all individual lives. Each individual has his period of destitution like any other, exactly as the hour of liberation is guaranteed to him. There was even-handed justice all round: but there was no fulfilment.

What valuation, then, has one to make of the case which has been persistently made on behalf of individual mystics or ascetics or even prophets? What is the meaning of the ever-persistent claim that there were men and women in human history well known for their spirit of detachment, perfect control over body and mind, and wholehearted and unstinted services to mankind without any expectation or return?

It would be stupid to suggest that such characters did not

exist except in the imagination of some foolish people. Nor would it be even commonsense to deny that a very hard and strenuous course of discipline preceded the achievement of ascetic greatness. And even if one makes a different assessment of the mystical or ascetic achievement from that which has been made by the believers in mysticism, there is no reason why one should miss the simple fact that the Mystics, like the Humanists, lived as historical beings and contributed, at least equally towards building up what we call civilization. Besides, it is well known that they did develop a detachment of spirit and yet most graciously served their fellow human beings as a matter of choice. It would be perverse to ignore these great achievements or to describe the long and arduous discipline that preceded them as primitive and barbarous. Besides, there is no record on the side of the Humanist which can beat it or which could not be equally ignored if we chose to be hostile.

But the question arises whether one could with any reason accept at their face value these arduous ascetic achievements? Did these achievements mean that the ascetics solved the problem of life and attained perfect peace and complete freedom from any form or shape of conflict?

The question is by no means simple and the complication is due to the fact that it is difficult to assess the meaning of perfect peace or complete freedom or life which an individual can legitimately claim. One can easily distinguish between peace and discord or freedom and slavery or the life of an individual and communal life. And it would be ridiculous to suspect that an ascetic never had peace of mind or freedom or a sense of individuality. In fact, by common consent, he leads a truly detached life with control over body and mind. Such a life stands out by way of sharp contrast to the life which the rest of the community actually live. Those, at any rate, who are engaged in warfare or serious conflicts with their fellow human beings cannot possibly be confused with the ascetics, who would gladly even offer their lives as a sacrifice rather than fight or resist to preserve them. Literally, there is no earthly interest of any great importance which weighs with them. The story of Alexander in India in the fourth century BCE as it has come down to us in Greek records is a very vivid or typical case in point.

But is there sufficient evidence in such cases of detachment or control to testify to the presence of perfect peace in them? If the peace of the ascetic never could be guaranteed except by the suppression of the opposite creed, should ascetic peace be still called perfect and pure? Could ascetic services, again, make up for this deficiency even if they were rendered as a matter of choice? The fact is that such services either never heal the wound which the ascetic creates in the Humanist or deaden the last lingering spirit of humanism. No doubt, the community takes on a homogeneous form under mystical control, with prospects of universal blessedness and peace, but it is equally completely bereft of humanistic joy. In no sense can the peace of the ascetic be called pure or perfect since it is bought by the price of the sorrow and slavery in the humanistic world. And every ascetic sooner or later realizes this superb piece of capricious irony in our human experience.

What again can one say about the duration of the peace which the ascetic enjoys? It comes after a life of hard discipline and rigorous practices; to be orthodox it does not arrive before the fourth stage of life falls due. Judged by the standard of duration alone it is very short-lived indeed and many a serious mind would question its supreme value simply because it is not lasting. A good many again, would strongly disapprove of it on the ground that it is the result of nothing but a long and strenuous fight or warfare with what we call passions or desires. A peace that is, frankly, the result of warfare in any form or shape cannot be true peace. There must necessarily be something abnormal in it since it was at least preceded by a destruction of values which were strictly opposed to the ascetic code. And it is too late in the day to dispose of "desires" and "passions" as if they were black goats specially created by God for sacrificial ends. To destroy or suppress a desire or passion is literally to destroy or suppress the individual or individuals who stimulated them. Not even the struggle with desires and passions as such in which the ascetic may be involved takes place wholly within the chamber of the ascetic mind. Whatever the value or significance of the inner struggle of any mind, it never occurs unless there is some other mind which bears the counterpart of the same struggle. While the ascetic is meeting ruthlessly the demand of his passion for beauty it follows necessarily that at least one beautiful woman is called upon to face complete destitution of her love or claim to beauty. While the ascetic's passion goes the way of doom under the rigour of the ascetic's discipline, the woman's love for beauty also goes the same way and as a result of the same rigour. The universe, then, by a strange nemesis, has only the peace of the ascetic to celebrate and in that celebration it is not beauty but its direct opposite, whatever that may be, that presides if the Humanist is allowed to comment on it. What then, in any case, is the value and texture of the peace which the Mystic enjoys?

Could, again, the purity and perfection of peace be secured unless there were a definite provision for the realization of both the values: that for which the ascetic stood and that which the beautiful woman most ardently espoused? If, however, there was nothing to choose between the values, whether of unity or freedom, it followed that either both had to be equally realized to guarantee peace or neither of them should be realized. And it would not be mis-stating history to say that neither the ascetic nor his rival the beautiful woman of tradition ever attained any peace. While the one proverbially made life as lean as he could do so that no beauty could germinate in it, the other made it wildly vivacious so that it soon became infested and poisonous in its growth. Peace there was none; but there was the assurance that one had given a quietus to one's opponent. There was a sense of freedom and liberation and nothing more.

And even this assurance did not last for ever. It lasted just long enough to complete the discomfiture of the opposite side. By the time their whole structure of civilization was not only pulled down but replaced by its opposite pattern, it was time for the "assurance" to dissolve. There was nothing permanent about it nor any sign of positive fulfilment.

Can we still claim that the supreme phenomenon, the unruffled and undisturbed calm of the ascetic was a value if we have to admit that it was at the expense of the peace and happiness of the Humanist?

There would be point in this claim if it could be proved that the Humanist had no value of his own which was on a par with that of the Mystic, or that he professed an end or objective which was the direct opposite of value. There have been attempts to discredit the Humanist as either the Evil Incarnate or at least a prototype of the primitive and uncouth. These, however, are but challenges which all claims in their dogmatic and absolute forms hurl at one another. They do not survive their sober moods in which they cherish, at least, some kind of recognition of one another. In any case, it is too late in the twentieth century to make a fetish of mysticism at the expense of humanism, as if freedom and individuality had no value whatsoever.

How then can the unruffled and undisturbed calm of the ascetic be regarded as value if it really means a death blow to the cause of freedom and independence? Or if we have to accept it as value not only because it is an unusual experience but, at least, an alleged solution of life's problems, what kind of value may it be?

Most unmistakably the unruffled moment of the Mystic is the moment of his complete triumph over humanism which to him is a real danger to the spirit, claimed to be the only truth or principle of life. It is a moment when neither body nor mind, the demons of the ascetic world, have a sway over him. There was no potency in them which could possibly distract him from his spiritual goal or draw him into awkward entanglements. He would not be persuaded by them, whatever their devices, to engage in conflicts or to undergo privation of the spirit. Proverbially, the ascetic stands firm in spite of all seductions, ready even to give up his life if needed, not to talk of credit, merit or authority. No power on earth, whatever its weapon, whether violence in its most concentrated shape or persuasion as the most seductive witchery ever known, can shake him.

Not to call this state of detachment an achievement or triumph would be a travesty of reason. The world, at any rate, literally bows to the detached ascetic and in some mood even worships him as God or appeases him by all means at its disposal lest his wrath might fall upon its head.

But does it follow that this superb ascetic triumph had, in fact, the very core of strength in it? Can it be claimed that it was all strength and nothing but strength and had none of the deficient and weak in its make-up? Can it be argued again that the ascetic could from the moment of that triumph live for ever as only the God or the gods were supposed to have lived? Does the strength which was behind this superb triumph of the ascetic over his enemies, the body and mind, augur well for an eternity of peace?

The answer is in the negative. At least historically, no such triumph ever endured long enough to bless the community at large. Whatever good or fulfilment of life it might have meant for the ascetic, it did not ensure a lasting peace in the human home. History, at any rate, is clear evidence that the achievements of the ascetics mark only steps in its career which disappear periodically, as steps on the sand dunes do, and their places, ere long, are taken by the steps or stages of humanism, their direct opposite. There has been, as yet, no permanent defeat of humanism at the hands of mysticism even as humanism has never failed to score a triumph over mysticism at the same rate and in exactly the same seasons as mysticism has over humanism.

The fact is that history till now has been mostly a venue in which the only truth that ever appeared was justice which guaranteed equal and mutual frustration of the Mystic and the Humanist. The fulfilment of the values which they stood for unmistakably is still in the lap of the gods.

But why did the ascetic fail to make his triumph complete? Where was the lack of strength in him or his creed?

There was a clear lack of strength or deficiency in the Mystic, and this deficiency appeared in him side by side with his peculiar strength. While he had unbounded faith in the Spirit which the Humanist did not possess, he had, strangely enough, no conception of what the Spirit really meant or was. The Spirit that he knew was in violent conflict with the Body which the Humanist upheld and so could not but be an illusion of the Spirit or a mere interpretation of it which was liable to be challenged. This was his chief and main deficiency.

The second deficiency was that he had neither faith in nor the conception of Body which was a value at least on a par with the Spirit. His conception of value, therefore, in spite of a profound faith in Spirit, was deficient and incomplete. He did not realize that there was a duality of values.

The third deficiency was that he took what was after all a technique of living, the point of which was to achieve liberation from bondage to which he was subject, or to inflict bondage on his opponent belonging to an opposite society, as the actual realization of the life of the Spirit.

One could easily point out that there were at least three corresponding deficiencies on the humanist side although they were of the opposite type. The Humanist had faith in Body, unlike the Mystic, but he had no conception of what Body truly was since the Body that he knew and stood for was in violent opposition to the Spirit which the Mystic upheld. Values which are opposed to one another as contraries or contradictories cannot but be illusions, since truth neither can nor does clash either with illusion or falsehood, not to say with truth. It is only illusions that can and do clash, and wherever there are clashes and conflicts it follows that there must be illusions between which the clash occurs. If the Mystic and the Humanist, therefore, actually and repeatedly clashed, at least their views could not but be illusions, they could not be truths. And it makes no difference even if one has to recognize that both of them had deep faith in Spirit and Body, respectively.

As regards the second deficiency it is evident that while the Mystic was oblivious of the Body or the fundamental claim of individuality, the Humanist was innocent of the Spirit or the fundamental claim of universalism. It never seriously struck the Mystic that the claim of individuality was just as ultimate and essential as the claim of universality. And exactly the opposite mistake was made by the Humanist who had no idea of the ultimacy of unity or universalism. Both suffered from deficiency since neither of them was in a position to appreciate the duality of values.

And from these two initial deficiencies followed the third in so far as they took it for granted that either the humanistic type of social system or the mystical social scheme was after all the embodiment of the Body or Spirit as they truly are. It did not strike them that as they were trying not only to establish one value instead of both the values, but also only the illusory interpretation of it, the constitution which embodied the fruit of that effort could achieve no result but mutual frustration. It has never been seen that whether one deals with the group scheme of society or its direct opposite, the individualistic scheme, one is not dealing with a social scheme which embodies Spirit and Body as they are: the two social schemes represent only or wholly two processes — liberation from bondage and infliction of bondage. The Mystic by his hierarchic system puts disabilities on the life of the Humanist, while the Humanist by his equalitarian system puts disabilities on the life of the Mystic. Here is a clash between two illusory interpretations of Spirit and universalism, and of Body and individualism; and the total result is the alternate appearance of the two opposite social schemes which ultimately disappear into scepticism. Neither Spirit nor Body survives, even as illusion, and in the long run there is never any social scheme to embody true Spirit or Body or anything like a fulfilment of them.

I have deliberately kept clear of any logical issue, though at each step I could not help drawing upon metaphysical conclusion. The evidence, however, on which I have drawn is derived almost altogether from historical facts or accepted opinion. There is no reason why one should deny the fact that the Mystic and the Humanist instead of co-operating in our tradition perpetually clashed. Nor is it necessary to dispute the logical implication of conflict as such — that it must at least imply contraries and contradictories in turn. The additional statement, that truth cannot clash with truth or with falsehoods or illusions, need not suggest any departure from traditional experience. Only it was high time one made it with precision or made explicit what had been implicitly held.

These, however, are sufficient grounds to support my claim that the mystical value like its opponent, the humanistic, was bound to be illusory. Also, this was all the evidence that I needed to explain that the Mystic suffered from innate deficiency in spite of the fact that by his specific strength he stood periodically detached, and, giant-like, fought his antagonist with great success.

The claim, however, that the Mystic was unattached and indifferent to all interests that sway mankind, falls to the ground. If it be a fact that the Mystic is unattached to the interests which derive from the Body, it is not true that he is unattached to the demands of the Spirit. On the contrary, while he is ready even to give up his Body, he is much too firmly wedded to Spirit and Soul to be severed from them even for a moment. Death, to him, is not the loss of bodily life but that of the life of the Spirit. He bewails his lot like a child if he loses communion even for a moment with his God. On the other hand, the Humanist is equally unattached and indifferent to all interests that sway mankind if it so happens that he lives in a mystical age. The loss of Spirit and Soul is no loss to him and death to him is not the death of Spirit but of Body. Besides, he achieves this great strength to withstand the attraction of Spirit by superhuman effort. The record of humanism in its fight against the Mystic is by no means a less profound achievement than that of the ascetic in his fight against the Humanist. In both cases, restraint and sacrifice played a part on as huge a scale as possible, and there is nothing to choose between the greatness and austerity of the one school and that of the other. No ascetic suffered from privation to achieve his liberation from the Body more than a Humanist did in seeking freedom from the clutches of the Spirit. The warfares that intervened between the two moments of bondage and slavery on the one hand, and liberation and freedom on the other are well known in human history. There is no injunction in history that we should draw a line of invidious distinction between the restraint and sacrifice of either side. Nor would it be correct to say that while the Mystic renounced the joys of life and chose the life of abnegation, the Humanist simply scorned abnegation and chose the life of enjoyment. The truth is that both the Mystic and the Humanist chose both forms of life — renunciation and enjoyment. If the Mystic renounced the life of the Body, the Humanist renounced the life of the Spirit even as they chose the life of the Spirit and Body, respectively, to cultivate them, if possible for all time. There was nothing to choose between them from any point of view although they went of their own accord to walk in opposite ways. In both cases, as destiny would have it, it was an adventure in the darkness of illusion.

And yet this conclusion about them does not mean any reflection on either the Mystic or the Humanist or on the values that they respectively chose to espouse. No harm was or could be done to the values since both were illusions, and nothing better or worse could be achieved by the Mystic and the Humanist since they lived in a world which was set for conflict and nothing but conflict. The main issue of that world was not that either the Mystic or the Humanist should have, at any cost, to realize the values or reach fulfilment of them; the main issue was that they were destined to appear in the arena which was set cosmically for an Armageddon of values, and to meet with complete frustration. Cosmically speaking that was the best that could happen to them or to the illusions which they had to take as values. Literally, it was not open to them either to escape this frustration or to establish peace or permanence of either form of life. Instead they had to follow rigidly the course of justice and take their share of joys and sorrows in perfectly even proportion. That, at any rate, has been the cosmic code so far and there was profound meaning in it if we go deep into its metaphysical implications.

If, again, we choose to review also their achievement in the field of speculation, the conclusion will be exactly the same. The God or the Absolute of the Mystic was by no means a more consistent or complete conception than the God who appeared in the shape of "Perpetual Becoming" as if by humouring to keep the Humanist in peace. If both claimed eternity on the strength of their Divinities both failed to achieve it since neither of the two Divinities succeeded in maintaining or preserving its own integrity. Since the mystical and humanistic divinities were frankly opposed to one another, their prospects lay only in a final exit from the field of speculation along with their votaries, the Mystic and the Humanist.

Whether, therefore, as unattached and unruffled figures of human history or as protagonists of divinities which served as the basis or source of their strength and which gave them periodically undisputed sway over their environment, the Mystic and the Humanist did not fare as they believed that they did. Whether, again, they rose high to power or authority or fell to bondage or slavery by turns, they served only illusions of values and never had a chance to stabilize their prospects.

And this is precisely the meaning underlying the claim to dual frustration which was made by Bapuji with regard to the whole of what we call history. At any rate, there is nothing in the mystical tradition to contradict this claim. It did not achieve any positive result; its achievement lay wholly in the dual process of inflicting disabilities on the Humanist and liberating itself from the bondage which the Humanist had imposed on it. And even this achievement could not escape the stage of scepticism into which both the Mystic and the Humanist fell as a matter of course.

VI

Atoms: The Duality of the Unique

If neither mysticism nor humanism can be credited with positive achievements sufficient to counteract the claim that history produced nothing but negative results, does it follow that our Bapuji, after his death, only repeated the sceptical conclusion which stood for inaction in life and negated all claim for values? If he had no reason to espouse either of the two dogmatic positions by virtue of the fact that between them, his life and death embodied dual frustration, was it necessary that there should be no alternative for him but to relapse into the position of the third figure in human history, the Sceptic?

My answer is that he did not represent any of these classical figures; he was not a dogmatist or a Sceptic. Perhaps there was no type in history which can serve as a parallel to the one which accrued to him after death. As in his life he was a figure by himself since his life in tune with the spirit of the age in which he lived was one continuous experiment with tradition, after his death he literally became a believer without any alignment with the Mystic or Humanist. It will be a mistake to judge him by what he said or did in his life as if he was only carrying out the command of the ages that had gone before him. With all his humility and self-surrender to Divinity, he remained right up to the end a figure whose sole aim in life was to put to the test the rich precepts of his heritage handed down from age to age. And at least some evidence for this claim can be derived from the miraculous manner in which death came to him. His experiment failed; the hypothesis did not work out. His self-surrender did not bring Divinity to earth, and so unity and love did not knit together the scattered creatures fighting darkness. There is no other explanation of the meaning of his death. If there was no slip of lapse in the ritual of worship, there was no hanging back from the sacrifices demanded, however arduous. The fifty years almost literally stood up as one perfect monolith of prayer in which homage was done to Divinity on an altar which was raised by the accumulated efforts of a galaxy of seers, prophets and thinkers before him. There was no foreign matter in the purity of the milk which was daily and even hourly offered as oblation to the spirit of the universe. The death was pre-determined; the universe had to change its whole behaviour. And so the last experiment had to be made; and after that there was no room for either dogmatism or scepticism. It was time for belief, construction and a fulfilment of the promise which lay deep in the heart of the universe. Gandhi, after his death, was the embodiment of that belief and the message which constituted it is the burden of my theme in the concluding portion of this little homage of mine to his memory as he lived for us on earth.

The core of that belief, as I see it, which suffused Gandhi after death is that there is a universe which made the conflict between the Mystic and the Humanist not only possible but absolutely essential. The dual frustration which embodied his life and death pointed to such a universe as its ultimate and necessary presupposition.

One may still hold that Bapuji was not aware of this universe either in his life when he made his heritage free or in his death which witnessed the demise of love. It was only after he had the full view almost as a historian of the new age of what had happened in his life and death that he recognized that universe.

And it is this discovery which gave a quietus to the long dream of the Sceptic who made it a point to try and replace the claim of Reality by that of the Negative. No longer was it possible for the Sceptic to urge that there was no Reality, on the ground that there was nothing to choose between the mystical and humanistic claims. The sceptical contention, which firmly held "evidence" to be the *sine qua non* of validity and succeeded in prevailing against the dogmatist, no longer stood. The universe that Gandhi discovered supplied the final evidence against scepticism that had so far been lacking in tradition. The Sceptic had now to retire for good.

The argument was that if dual frustration was a fact and if both values which were professed by the Mystic and the Humanist suffered from mutual neutralization, at least neutralization remained as fact to be accounted for. The act or event of failure to prove that reality was mystical or humanistic did not imply a disproof of its own existence. If again that failure, after having embodied the self-contradiction of either view of reality, completed itself in confusion or doubt in which both the views stood out as contraries, still the fact of doubt or confusion remained to be accounted for. There was at least the Sceptic to vouchsafe for its reality. The fact or state of doubt could not possibly be equated with the Absolute Negative, or most fatefully even the sceptical function would have lapsed. It should be easy to see that if there was only the Absolute Negative, there would be no occasion for the Sceptic either to prove the reality of doubt or to disprove the dogmatist. The universal assumption was that the "disproof" was a fact and that a claim for the Negative was made. And once this assumption arose, scepticism could not cut into the roots of reality altogether. All that was possible at its hands as a calamity was that the Mystic and the Humanist of history, or history as known so far, would altogether lose their claim to recognition. And that was exactly what took place in the appearance of the meteoric phenomenon — dual frustration. It gave a burial to all the three figures of history — the Mystic, the Humanist and the Sceptic.

But what would or could be the nature of a universe which made conflict and its inevitable result possible and even necessary? Why, again, should such a universe be considered necessary? Could not conflict between types of values, theories, and actions take place without any third entity either upholding them or creating them or serving them as an ideal?

There is, at any rate, a claim in the scientific world that entities, whether one calls them by the name of atoms or that of their near or distant progenitors, attract and repel one another in space or some other medium which is supposed not to affect seriously the conflict between them. What is implied is that a third entity is not necessary to account for either the existence of the multiple atoms or entities or the way in which they act or react upon one another. Space or ether, or any another medium which may make movement in direction possible, may be assumed as playing some part in this primal situation. But somehow this additional entity is not believed to be a determinant factor in the same way as the atoms are believed to be. At any rate, one does not know if space or ether undergoes the experience of attraction and repulsion itself as atoms do, or if the atoms are attracted and repelled by space and ether exactly as they are attracted and repelled by one another. It is a different issue whether space and ether should have been assumed as an additional factor in the main drama of conflict between the atoms, even though they do not attract and repel like the atoms.

This is not the place to raise a scientific issue; but I have to draw the attention of the scientific world to this curious hypothesis about space and ether which implies all the difficulties connected with the notion of passivity and yet does not seem to contribute to the main drama in any real sense. It is difficult to see how anything real whether it is active or passive, could help being an entity, and yet if it has to be an entity, its place must be on a par with that of the atoms. At any rate, the conflict can no longer be confined to only two types of atoms but must imply at least three.

But can conflict possibly appear between three entities if it has to be between contradictories and contraries? What then is the function of space or ether in a drama of conflict between atoms? It is conceivable that the atoms may be involved in a downpour of conflict. As if the bed of the universe was a vast stretch of swamp in which the atoms were drenched and soaked in marshy conflict. But even such a wet, slippery universe would have to make room for two distinct types of aquatic atoms like full-grown walruses squirting muddy water on one another. No universe, whatever the extent or degree of the conflict which raged among its constituents, could escape some order or other in that conflict. The constituents had to appear in two distinct blocs or sides; there had to be a duality or dichotomy in their arrangement. Where then does the third type of atom come in? If again, space or ether or direction have to be recognized as facts of experience, they too will have to face conflicts in which "spaces", "directions" and "ethers" take part like the atoms. And in such conflicts there would be naturally two types of "space", "ether" and "direction" side by side with the two types of atoms, protons, etc. Will this agree with the scientific dream?

It is another story, however, whether the claim on behalf of atoms that they are ultimate constituents would in any case stand. Even if space, ether, direction, etc., are added as additional entities to the main stock in which conflict in the sense of attraction or repulsion takes place, the issue will still arise whether the atoms or the spaces by themselves are capable of accounting for the conflict in the shape of attraction or repulsion. Is duality, in other words, capable by itself of accounting for conflict? Can two "atoms" or "spaces" or "directions" clash as contradictories or contraries simply because they exist as dual entities?

No doubt an atom cannot come into conflict with itself. But can it clash with another if only it be a fact that that atom exists exactly as it itself exists? Can mere existence of duality, i.e. can the fact that two atoms exist, instead of one, make at once a conflict possible or necessary between them? No doubt if one atom exists, so can two or any number at that rate, but it is one thing for atoms to exist, another thing for them to come into conflict with one another. Some factor or condition is necessary for the possibility of conflict between them in addition to their bare existence.

The issue, therefore, is what could be that factor or condition, an issue which it does not seem the scientist has raised with any seriousness.

The factor or condition in question presumably is what the well-known category of relationship implies. Unless the atoms not only exist but also stand in relationship to one another, conflict between them — it is immaterial whether one calls it by the name of attraction or repulsion or contradiction or contrariety — cannot possibly take place. They cannot attract or repel on another, or stand to one another as contradictories or contraries unless they both exist and actually stand related.

And this means that the atoms, by virtue of the fact that they stand related, have to exist in a form which is distinguishable from what is known as unique existence.

There are, indeed, two types of existence: first, one which the atom possesses on the ground of its being an atom, and for which it cannot be confused with any other; second, the other which the atom possesses on the ground of its being related to other atoms and on account of which it is at one with other atoms. The clash arises between two types of existence.

If, for instance, an atom lived its own life without any

relationship to any other atom, it would certainly be unique and nothing but unique. In this sense of uniqueness only the Divine person is unique, although it is quite another matter what form of individuality does and may accrue to the "universal" and the "absolute" which are also familiar ways of embodying the Divine. To many they are indistinguishable by virtue of their pervasive totality — a state or condition which cannot be demarcated from that of the absolute negative. There can be no question, however, that at least the Divine Personality does imply uniqueness — a feature which it was necessary for the human mind to conceive of by way of contrast to the indistinguishability of the absolute.

Yet, if the atoms do not by any chance reach up to the monistic altitude of the Absolute, but choose to stay on the plane of multiplicity, they may still preserve their uniqueness if it were possible that they could remain as absolute differents. There is no necessity for the absolutely different atoms to shed their uniqueness, or add to it the non-unique feature. Perhaps the humanistic ideal in its total aspiration reached the level of the absolute differents — a level in which each individual atom, perchance, could exist without any relationship to any other as a perfect God, living its own life unconcerned with anything that happened outside or in the wide realm of the divine multiple.

All such possibilities for unique existence, however, disappear as soon as atoms either choose or have to exist in relationship. Two distinct conditions of existence at once arise for them: first, they have to preserve their uniqueness which is due to their specific and distinguishable feature; second, they have to preserve also their relatedness or oneness with others which is due to their relationship. Every atom, somehow or other, has to exist and function as unique and distinguishable and also exist and function as at one with others.

It is the fact of relationship which accounts for the origin of what may be called the common character, oneness or identity with others, while the fact of distinguishability accounts for the unique feature and complete independence of every atom.

Yet this outstanding category of relationship has given rise to controversies in our philosophic tradition which still remain undecided. It is a familiar piece of our philosophic misfortune. The difficulties, however, that arose were due to the assumption that relationship is an additional fact to the terms or entities that are related. Nobody can miss this strange assumption.

My definition of it, however, departs from this usage altogether. To me only the entities or terms exist: nothing else does, not even the universals or what has been known as potentiality. I have discussed all this at length in my Metaphysic. But individuals must and do exist in forms which give full satisfaction for believing in relationship as a notion. The evidence for relationship appears in the particular form in which the individual exists and not in any additional existence distinguishable from that of the individual.

But the question arises why should atoms attract or repel one another or stand to one another as contradictories or contraries simply because it was not possible that they should exist without featuring both uniqueness and commonness in their identity? Could they not instead have harmonized and co-operated with one another?

The obvious answer is that the two features or the values that correspond to them stand as opposites to one another as a matter of historical fact. For an atom to be unique is for it to be the direct opposite of being common or identical. So far there have been no formulations of the categories, uniqueness and commonness, such as could resolve the opposition between them. No atom, therefore, could conceivably exist if it was necessary that it had to be both unique and common while existing in a society of atoms. An atom certainly could be unique if it lived by itself, but in a society of atoms it had to be common with others in addition to its being unique and distinguishable from them.

What then did or could happen to the atoms when they lived in a society? How would they exist in such a society, if it were not possible that both the features could be cherished by them at the same time? If, again, the society of atoms in any case had to be there — it had been there as a matter of historical fact — what was or could be ordained for the atoms so far as the features of their existence were concerned?

It had to be that the atoms should have to form two distinct and separate types of society in which either the one or the other feature happened to be emphasized at the expense of the other. There would also be two different types of atoms belonging to the two societies.

It may be disputed, however, that since the atoms were not rational beings, but just centres of energy, they were incapable of forming societies, or even if by some cosmic inadvertence they did form social organizations, such societies could not be of a dual type, but were bound to be homogeneous in their form. Such a contention will be perfectly in line with the main trend of scientific opinion, and except for stray philosophic claims and some forms of pantheistic faith, social claims for the atoms would go by the board.

I am not, however, arguing on the basis of either philosophic or scientific records. My main object is to complete the analysis which these records left unfinished. I do suggest that our scientists did not know all that the clash between the atoms implied as a matter of verifiable fact. They are not in a position to question the validity of my claim, which is based on evidence to which hitherto they have not had access; and since I do not deny their main contention that atoms do clash and attract and repel one another, it is for them to go over the ground with me and not be unnecessarily squeamish. As for the philosophers they have no case whatever, since they have achieved as the total result of their efforts nothing but an impasse in human thought.

But I do claim that the atoms form societies just as human beings do, and these societies are of a dual type exactly as human societies have ever been in the records of human history. There are two types of atoms as there are two types of human beings, and these types emphasize oneness at the expense of uniqueness, and also equally the reverse. And they constitute dual types of social schemes which may be described as group and individualist.

My suggestion is that from the point of view of social structure in which alone atoms can exist and function, there is nothing to choose between them and the human beings. Logically, there was no alternative except for them all to plunge into the abysmal depth of the Absolute Negative. The question of difference between the atoms and human beings with regard to the constitution in which they exist and function or to the nature of their bare existence does not arise. It arises in an altogether different field.

The dual societies of the atoms, however, if between them they preserved both the entities, the unique and the identical, could not guarantee peace or harmony between the atoms. Invariably the group societies of atoms came into clash with the individualistic society by virtue of their opposite professions. They frankly menaced one another, since they were out to realize altogether opposite objectives. If the success of the group society meant the elimination of the ideal of independence and uniqueness it could hardly be anything but fatal to the prospects of the individualistic society and vice versa.

And it is no good surmising a compromise on the basis, say, of sheer space and time: as if the two societies could occupy different parts of the globe and appear in different periods of time to fulfil their incompatible objectives. The minimum for which each society planned was a limitless fruition, neither space nor time could draw a limit to that fruition or plan. No ideal or aspiration, whatever its credential, could stand an initial limit to its final consummation. Historically it has taken the form either of the "mystical absolute" or "perpetual infinite".

Besides, the two societies had to belong to a universe and the universe had to be one, unless it chose to dally with the illusion of duality which, without relationship, was but another name for the indistinguishable or the absolute negative. The two societies had to belong to the same universe and naturally they were destined to come into clash at every step of their long career.

But the question arises, why should one presuppose a universe at all to account for the conflict between the two societies. Could not the two societies meet and clash without belonging to a third entity which we have called the universe? Could not the two societies be opposites without there being anything else, as it were, to bring them into opposition? Why should not contradictories and contraries just exist by themselves and clash?

The difficulty is that two societies, like two atoms, cannot clash or co-operate unless they are related. As absolute differents it was not possible that they should either clash or co-operate. And the fact that they are opposites is a proof that they are at least related, which means that in spite of their mutual opposition they have something in common between them. If a conflict or clash between atoms or societies must imply relationship between them, it is inconceivable that they could be just contradictories or contraries without anything else between them to form their common identity.

The question therefore arises, could they be identical with one another and at the same time incompatibles and opposites?

The answer to it implies the fundamental issue whether one can conceive of entities which clash as contradictories or contraries except as determinates. We have to ask, for instance, if it is possible that atoms can be regarded as just attracting and repelling centres, as centres which simply undergo change. Will it be a sufficient and complete account of them if we just mark the changes that they undergo?

These questions imply an analysis of the notion of identity or the nature of an entity.

It is easy to see that every entity must have an identity of its own; that is the bare, ultimate necessity by the Law of Identity. But as all entities have to have sufficient "stuff" in their identity to escape being merged in the absolute negative, they cannot be indeterminate, but must have a determinate nature with a capacity to conceive and realize an end. The Law of Identity, i.e. "*A* is *A*" does not raise all these additional questions which refer to the nature of Identity. It is significant enough to distinguish the entity from the absolute negative since the latter has no identity. But it does not define what identity as a notion implies; or what the absolute negative as a notion excludes. Identity, to be precise, implies distinguishability as well as capacity to conceive an end or objective and to realize it. The absolute negative is not distinguishable nor is it capable of conceiving an end, or working it out.

In other words, three distinct features are implied by the nature or identity of an entity. In so far as the negative is indeterminate, indistinguishable and incapable of conceiving or realizing ends, every entity has to be determinate, distinguishable and capable of conceiving and realizing ends.

These are the ultimate minimum features without which the existence of an entity is not conceivable.

To think of an atom, for instance, as indeterminate in the sense that it is just a focal point in which somehow alternatives meet, is to think of it as non-existent. By the Law of Identity, every entity has to have a nature of its own — a condition which the notion of alternatives just neutralizes. The atom that is indeterminate must have alternative natures. It never crystallizes into definiteness — as if all the energy in the indeterminate state was spent in the preliminary attempt on the part of the opposites to fuse — which is an impossible feat. It was not for nothing, therefore, that some bold Ethicists and their collaborators, the Moralists, thought that one could choose between the opposites — a performance which, however conceivably necessary for practical purposes, produced only chaos in our social existence. Alternatives can be conceived of, but they are not capable of existing either as desires or as cosmic forces even though they might aim at the highly respectable ideal of building up God's creation. The atom or any entity or being cannot be indeterminate, it has to be determinate. It is only the Absolute Negative that can be indeterminate. Even God cannot be indeterminate, even to give a support to indeterminate ethics. An atom, again, has to be distinguishable, which means that it must be one among many. No entity except the Absolute can escape the necessity which multiplicity rigidly implies. It has to be in both the states: multiplicity and simplicity. And, of course, the Negative is indistinguishable since it is nothing.

But it is not enough that an atom or any other entity should be just determinate and distinguishable. It must be able also to conceive of an end and to realize it. A failure to conceive of an end or to work it out would at once relegate it to the limbo of the Negative. The Negative does not conceive of an end nor work it out.

There are at least two clear reasons why the notion of end goes with identity. First, since it is a conceivable notion, no entity can possibly be without it. Reality as distinguished from the Negative has to have every conceivable form of existence. It cannot go without any or choose to discard any. All possibilities have equally a claim to fruition. It would be a fatal deficiency in Reality if in it there was a lack of any possibility. Most indisputably reality which is not complete is at the mercy of the Negative. Second, existence implies perpetuity since the static or perfect is indistinguishable from the Negative. The notion of perpetuity, again, implies change which is never absent from existence or reality. In some sense or other it must imply a capacity to bring about changes without a limit. There could be no moment in reality lying stagnant and, therefore, no identity which is not active since the vacuum is the sphere of the Negative.

If by any chance this perpetual becoming is interfered with, there can be nothing to prevent the Negative from swamping the whole field of Reality. The heart of Reality, as we know it, is perpetual becoming, though in a sense undreamt of by our dynamic philosophers.

The conclusion is obvious that identity must imply the capacity to conceive end and to realize it.

If, however, every entity has to have an end or objective, with the capacity to realize it as well as a determinate and distinguishable nature of its own, it follows that the end has to be both unique and common, since no entity exists except in relation to other entities. If the notion of relationship must imply an existence for the entity in a form which implies oneness and commonness, it cannot conceive of an end except in both forms: common and unique.

If an atom, for instance, is in relation to some other atoms, it is not enough that it should be determinate and distinguishable from the other atoms, it must also cherish a common end with them. An atom cannot be considered without a common end.

To conceive of it as mere change without an end, therefore, will be meaningless, since as an existent entity it has to have an end. Besides, change which implies both previous and later changes cannot be accounted for without ends. It is an end which implies an effort to realize it. The effort has no meaning apart from the end, and since all changes are nothing but efforts — they cannot be supposed to be anything but efforts — changes must imply ends. Atoms as changes represent, at least, efforts and so they must imply a state in which they must have existed as conceiving ends.

To conceive of the atoms in an accurate or adequate way, therefore, we have to assume that they must have not only natures, ends and efforts to realize them but common and unique natures, ends and efforts. In other words, we have to consider them functioning in two successive states. In one they profess a common end and in professing it they appear with common natures and common efforts here is a distinct state or society of atoms and in this state or society the atoms live and function with a view to conceive the common end. The total result is the actual conception of the common end or ideal. The society now is fully aware of its ideal or end. In another state they profess distinct ends and appear with unique natures and act uniquely to realize that end. Here is also a distinct state or society of atoms, and in this state or society the atoms live and function if only to realize the common end. The total result, however, is a failure to realize the common end. This is not the sphere in which the common or identical in any sense appears.

Can it not be argued, then, that the atoms could be both identical with one another from the point of view of their natures, ends and efforts as well as different from one another?

If we accept the first state in which they conceive their common end, we should have no difficulty in accepting their identical and communal condition. Here they do exist as a harmonious body in which they co-operate to conceive their common end. They are identical in the sense that they conceive of the self-same end and all function together to make the conception of the common end possible.

But as in the nature of things, they have also to be unique in their natures, ends and efforts, differences arise between them when they proceed to realize the common end.

There will be in this period of their activity no such thing as common nature, common end or common effort. There will be instead two distinct natures, distinct ends and distinct efforts. The society of atoms and entities will be divided into two sections, each professing its own nature, end and the technique of realizing it. The two societies will be authoritarian or libertarian. And the clash will begin between them on the ground that from all points of view, i.e. nature, end and effort, the authoritarian and libertarian atoms stand out as incompatibles and opposites. There is nothing to choose between them. They clash either as contradictories or contraries.

An atom, for instance, which is authoritarian and professes oneness as its essential nature, has for its immediate object order or unity, and follows the technique of hierarchy. On the other hand, the libertarian atom has for its nature uniqueness and independence as the goal or objective and equalitarianism as the technique of realizing its objective.

And the reason why this division of the atoms takes place in the shape of two groups in the same society and with a conflict between them is dual:

1. Here is a sphere of existence which ruled out commonness in nature, end and effort and made

uniqueness the central feature. The atoms or entities in it existed as unique entities — a state in which there was room for as much difference between them as possible. Where there is room for differences, conceivably there is also room for all kinds of it, not excluding conflicts.

2. But since uniqueness by itself cannot constitute the identity or nature of any entity, no atom or entity can exist even in such a sphere of existence except in relation to other atoms. A society of atoms whatever its form has to have relationship as the main lever of its cohesion. The unique atoms have to stand related lest they be reduced to the state of absolute differents. There is no alternative to it, and so no question arises.

The duality of techniques in a society of atoms, therefore, necessarily arose. If the atoms or entities had to realize the common objective, there were two ways by which they could realize it: the way which is derived from the fact of relationship and the way which is derived from the feature of uniqueness. And since these two ways are incompatible with one another, the atoms had to split into sections and adopt one or the other technique. Here arise in a simultaneous form both the techniques although in two opposite groups.

Duality, therefore, forms the very keynote of the "unique". There can be no question that duality embodies the unique and that alone, it is by no means capable of being confused with the "common" or "identical". There was no duality in the sphere when the ideal was conceived. None of the three features of existence in that sphere — end, effort and nature — partook of the dual character. The whole community of atoms when the "conception of the ideal" took place was one compact body with a common goal, nature and effort. And this feature of commonness changed into duality as soon as the state of conception changed into the state of realization.

And yet there is no room for doubt that duality can provide for uniqueness, when the atoms or entities which constitute the community have to be multiple. The doubt would be relevant if multiplicity were conceived in the form or shape of absolute differents. If the atoms or entities could not be unique unless they were totally unrelated, duality of nature could not provide for or safeguard their uniqueness. And one may incidentally refer to the humanistic conception of each individual attaining self-sufficiency as an evidence of the presumption that nothing short of absolute differents or non-relation can be a guarantee for uniqueness. If, however, a state of absolute differents or non-relatedness is inconceivable as an existent state, the notion of uniqueness necessarily must go with the notion of relatedness. The unique has to be related to other uniques. It would be enough for its preservation as unique if only it could avoid the common or identical. And duality is exactly that state which provides for it. In so far, therefore, as the sphere of realization provides for a dual nature, dual objective and dual technique, it provides for the uniqueness of the atom.

May we not conclude then that there was a state in which the atoms or entities exist and function which is not to be confused with the state in which they attract or repel one another? Should it not be held that the atoms exist in two states instead of the one in which the scientists have so far studied them and that these two states are essentially related to one another?

It is time that the scientists and other thinkers realized that unless the common end or objective is conceived in a state in which the society of atoms held together in perfect harmony there would be no occasion for the atoms to clash or attract or repel one another. There would be no drama of conflict, whether in the strictly atomic world or any other world which lies close to its boundary.

And this is what was meant when we posited, as an article of Bapuji's faith, a third entity or a universe as a presupposition of the conflict of values and theories. And perhaps the Chinese philosopher too meant the same thing when he in his cryptic, aphoristic way claimed that if there was a bay horse and a dun cow, there was bound to be a third thing. There can be no question that a drama of conflict which embodies two distinct beliefs and values, held by two distinct societies, must presuppose as its basis or support another drama in which the ideal or main purpose was conceived in perfect harmony and amity.

In common language, disagreement in any context implies an agreement in another context which is directly implied by it. There has, at least, to be an agreement about an ideal before disagreement can arise in the course of realizing the ideal. If, by any chance, the agreement had not arisen, there would be no occasion for disagreement since nothing takes place in a vacuum. If conflict and disagreement have to be taken as positive facts, agreement about the basis or implication of conflict has to be taken as equally positive. We have to agree with our opponent as to what should be the aim of our life before we are fated to run counter to one another in our very normal attempt to realize that aim. Agreement and disagreement, in the nature of things, imply one another, however paradoxical it may sound.

VII

Possibility of the Absolute

What then is the nature of the universe which was implied in the belief of our Bapuji as the basis or presupposition of the perpetual conflict between the Mystic and the Humanist? Could it be described in terms of any of the universes we have hitherto known and believed to be real?

The universes so far known are all classifiable under the two heads: mystical and humanistic. We have not been familiar with any universe except that of the Mystic in which the multiple constituents appear for a time and then are gathered into the monistic compass of the indescribable Absolute, or that of the Humanist in which the multiple equally appears for a time, although related in an aggregate of unique particulars, and then raised by sheer individual aspiration to a state in which the unique becomes self-sufficient and enjoys the free and unregulated opportunity to "become" in perpetuity.

Neither of these two universes can be a model or prototype of the third universe which Gandhi discovered after his death, for the simple reason that it is these universes which formed the constituents of the drama of conflict and came to grief in the life and death of Gandhi. They were the landmarks of frustration in human history; one cannot confuse the very source of frustration with frustration itself.

It has to be noted that, so far in human history, nothing but a drama of conflict between two universes formed either a symbol or picture of the universe or the universe itself. No historian ever recorded an account of a universe that was stable, although both the Mystic and the Humanist persistently claimed that it was their specific universe which was the only stable and real universe. What unmistakably went to constitute the clash of history and what the historians duly recorded were only theories and beliefs about universes and not universes as objective facts. And if the theories and beliefs were facts and not legends or fictions, they did not exhaust the possibilities nor by any means provide for stability. The universe that we have so far consciously belonged to and taken to be the only real, objective universe was of our own making and did not exist outside our experiences. There was nothing which could be called objective corresponding to our experiences; the only things objective were the experiences themselves. And if there was no other universe upholding the drama of conflict between the two types of experiences which we called by the name of universe, the "dual frustration" was sure to have brought the whole of reality within the ambit or orbit of the Absolute Negative. Today, we should be literally floating in the transparent emptiness of the real negative, peaceful but completely and hopelessly dead.

It is against such a grim eventuality that the belief in a universe which Bapuji conveyed to me made a true and rock-like stand. No other message could have left the prospects of the human race surviving today. If mankind had to take his death as final, it would have instantly and irretrievably perished. Like chaff before the wind, the whole universe would have vanished. That, at any rate, is the only logical conclusion.

But what exactly was the message about that universe? What is its nature? How does it come into the life that we actually live? The issue that arises refers to a reality that was not discussed in any philosophic or prophetic tradition. The universe in question was not held as part and parcel of the remote realm of the mystical dream, nor did it glow at the far end of the humanistic goal. These universes, as I have already suggested, did not reach out to the objective world after their inception in the human mind, in spite of the fact that profound faith and arduous practices nourished them. Even the glow of mystery shed round them by their strange, limitless prospect did not evolve any objectivity in them.

Unlike them, the universe which is the one presupposition of the drama of conflict between the two known universes of history is frankly and indisputably objective. If human mind can conceive of it, that conception is not what constitutes its identity. It exists by its own right and quite independently of that conception.

What, however, distinguishes it from the universe of history is not so much the fact that, unlike them, it is not subject to changes which provided for their career nothing but a steady flow of conflict; the distinguishing feature of this universe appears in the conception of the ideal which it holds firmly in a state of perfect agreement. It is a universe in which nothing happens but the act of conceiving the ideal which is presupposed by the drama of conflict. Realization is not its theme. What is more, the ideal that is conceived is nothing like what ideals have been considered to be in the historic record of the drama of conflict. In fact, the only category which can accurately describe it is Possibility of the Absolute, a category which was not formulated in the whole vocabulary of our philosophic or prophetic tradition. There has been no instance of it in human experience, and the reason for its universal absence is that tradition understood the categories of the Absolute and Possibility in senses which clearly excluded the chances of any fusion between them. It would be ridiculous to say that the Absolute and Possibility of tradition were altogether irresponsible hypotheses, as the humanists and pluralists were inclined to urge. In fact, both terms can equally be traced in the pluralistic conception of Infinite Becoming.

But neither usage would lend itself to a combination of the kind I have suggested in the Possibility of the Absolute. And if I succeeded where others failed, the source of my good fortune lay in the discovery of quite unorthodox ideas about the terms "Absolute" and "Possibility". What they are has been elaborately discussed in *The Real and the Negative*. There is nothing forbidding about them provided the reader sees the main point of my metaphysical position.

It might, however, appear odd that I should have to use abstruse metaphysical categories to draw out the implication of Bapuji's message, which, in spite of his dialectical mind, he might never have contemplated. The responsibility is mine and I take it with the full assurance that there was no other way to interpret his message. The procedure, however unusual, does not entail even an apology on my part.

There is no reason, however, why I should not confess that a wholly original metaphysical position is presupposed by the category which I have described as "Possibility of the Absolute". My claim is that if I have to accept the message of Bapuji, orientated from the dual frustration in his life and death, there is no alternative to my formulating that metaphysic. In fact, the historian of the future is bound to note that what I came to uphold as a matter of sheer logical thought was verified to the hilt by action spread over half-a-century in the life of Gandhi. The two events, without any direct or intimate contact in their origin, practically fused. Would it be odd if I introduced my philosophic position as the implication of Gandhi's life-long experiment?

Any serious treatment of that position, however, in a treatise like this is quite out of the question. The most that may be attempted, as a matter of bare introduction, is a very broad statement, and that, too, for the sole purpose of softening the abstruseness of a category like the Possibility of the Absolute.

Reality to me is a duality in which the terms alternate instead of being simultaneous, a completely unorthodox claim.

The terms are "Absolute" and the "Possibility of the Absolute". In other words, Reality exists, either as the Absolute or as the Possibility of the Absolute. It is never the Absolute only or just its Possibility. The relation between them is one of implications and that condition only means that both are equally necessary if Reality has to be, rather than the Negative.

This broad statement, however, does not go into the question of the meaning of the two terms, "Absolute" and "Possibility of the Absolute", nor does it define the category "Possibility of the Absolute". I have to refer my readers to *The Real and the Negative* for a full and elaborate discussion on all the implications.

It will be found that the Absolute and Possibility of the Absolute are two different realms. Their constitution and achievement do not coincide. In fact, what happens in the Possibility of the Absolute is a dual phenomenon, "doubt about the Absolute" and "certainty about the Absolute". Reality exists as Absolute, and this phase alternates with another phase in which doubt and certainty about the Absolute appear in succession. In simple language, there is either the Absolute functioning or the Possibility of the Absolute functioning, i.e. there is either the Absolute or Doubt followed by Certainty about the Absolute.

This is a very different account from any which we have inherited from tradition and on which we are still busy improvising variations. I cannot expect my readers will see the difference unless they make themselves familiar with my main position. But I have to introduce all this unusual metaphysic in my attempt to interpret Bapuji's message, since there is no alternative. There is no philosophic or prophetic tradition which will account for the implication of that "dual frustration"; and I have, at least, the consolation that I have not used any esoteric or legendary tradition to establish my position.

VIII

The Society of Beings

If the Possibility of the Absolute rather than the Absolute has to be taken as the ideal, what follows is that there should be two distinct stages with regard to it: first, a stage which will embody the act of conceiving it, second, a stage which will introduce the act of realizing it. Realization of it would be inconceivable if it had not been already conceived as an ideal. And no conception of it would be possible if, in the nature of things, realization of it were impossible. The processes of conception and realization imply one another and are meaningless in isolation.

The conclusion that follows is momentous; the world to which we belong must have begun in a stage in which the Possibility of the Absolute was conceived, which means that there must have been a "society of beings" in its initial stage which fulfilled the essential need of achieving a conception of it. One cannot possibly overrate or exaggerate the significance of this truth.

And it is this stage in the career of our universe, which Bapuji referred to by implication as the basis or presupposition of the drama of conflict, which ended in dual frustration in his life. Here is the third thing of the Chinese philosopher and the fresh discovery which was implied in the comments which Bapuji made to me.

Yet there is nothing extra logical in my conclusion about the existence of a "society of beings" which initiated the universe and never left it lest the whole universe might collapse for the lack of an ideal; it is strictly derived from logical bases. If we have to accept dual frustration as fact, there is no help for us except to presuppose the "society of beings" as the basis or ground of that fact. Neither dogmatism, whether of the mystical or humanistic type nor scepticism, which rears itself on a detail of human experience, can bar the way. They are outworn with age-old, fruitless efforts either to affirm reality without evidence or to deny reality simply because there was no evidence. Bapuji's "society of beings" is not like any society of spirits that we have on record whether vouchsafed for by some kind of testimony or simply believed in as the primal factor in the regulation of cosmic laws. All such societies of spirits traced their origin to one or another of the two main stocks of history — the mystical or the humanistic. They can have no possible alignment with the "society of beings" since it was the presupposition of both the mystical and humanistic stocks of history.

But how is this discovery to be utilized for social purposes? If we have no direct touch with the "society of beings", is it possible that we can draw help from it to make life grow again on our social soil? Is there any indication in this logical discovery that the field where the dual frustration took place may again be revitalized and that in a way which will not just repeat the cycle of the drama of conflict?

There is, at least, one way in which the discovery can be utilized almost at once, not only to reform the constitution of our social scheme but also radically to change the technique or mode of running it. We can, if we follow its structure and achievement, abolish the two methods of active and passive warfare and build up a social economy which will call for co-operative and harmonious effort to achieve common results. Besides, there is a clear indication in this discovery that such a change has fallen due. And the reason why I am making this unusual though sorely needed claim is simple.

The "society of beings", if we have to admit its validity, whether it has so far been recognized or not, is at least an existent society, which means that the beings who constitute it exist in relationship to one another and bring about by their harmonious and co-operative functions a definite and determinate result. They succeed in conceiving the ideal of the relative world — the Possibility of the Absolute.

It is a different issue how that ideal is conceived or what exactly it is. Since we as human beings do not belong to that society it is open to us only to believe that such events happen. We cannot visualize the nature of that happening nor formulate the full significance of it.

The moral, however, that one can draw from this strictly logical situation is that a harmonious and co-operative society is possible as an existent fact side by side with another society which may be steeped in conflict. If it be true that human history has been nothing but conflict, it is also true that while we human beings have known nothing in our long history but conflict, there have been other beings who lived a life of pure harmony and peace. And what is more, that life of harmony was essential for even the possibility of our life of conflict, whether we knew about it or not. In other words harmony and conflict both belonged to the same universal scheme; and one can, at least, argue that we human beings from our very inception have been equally and essentially involved in both harmony and conflict.

The moment, however, arrived after the dual frustration in the life and death of Bapuji when the issue of conflict in, at least, a logical sense simply dropped out and the need arose for assessing the social value of harmony and that alone. There can no longer be any significant claim left in conflict as a mode of living since the two ideas and values which made conflict both possible and necessary are literally lying dead.

The alternatives, therefore, are either clean scepticism, which stands for "complete inaction" both in thought and practice or "action" on a plane where truths and values fully harmonize instead of clashing. And it is the second alternative that has fallen due by the discovery of Bapuji in the light of which it should be legitimate for us to concentrate on our common interests and subordinate all confiicts to that universal accord. If the "society of beings" could live conceiving the ideal — such a life had to be lived whether for the universe or the human race — it should be possible for us too to live wholly for conceiving our ideal. It may even be urgent that we should have to work together for our common interests and postpone the function of realizing our ideal goal to a distant future. We have at least to preserve ourselves and make sure about the ideal for which to work. There is no alternative to this procedure.

Besides, it is a historical fact that there has been no society or State which did not live at least half the time in doing nothing but conceiving its ideal. No ancient or modern State had to spend all its energies in organizing external or internal warfare. On the contrary, in every society or State there were common interests to realize; there was such a necessity as preservation of the people or society. Not indeed before a society reached the stage when it was time for it to decline would it fail to draw a line between the two functions of preserving a society and giving its members every possible chance to engage in conflicts if only to realize its common goal. There is such a thing as conceiving the ideal for which the society or State stands and by which alone its decision is taken as to which other State or States should be its normal ally or foe. Technically all the work done in the name of the preservation of common interests comes under the heading "conceiving the ideal".

The issue therefore arises, in what way exactly should we

change the function of the State with reference to the two distinct objectives: first, conceiving the ideal or preservation of the common interest, second, creating opportunities for regulated fighting to determine which of the two ways of realizing the ideal is the right one. The answer is simple and clear. If we have to drop the second function as useless and harmful — we cannot go on fighting as democrats and autocrats since both values and techniques have been proved to be equally illusory — there is no occasion for dropping the first. Instead, most certainly, there is every reason for emphasizing its value and importance.

If, for instance, the Socialist and the Conservative in Britain today are proved to be equally wrong in their conflicting estimates of the British technique of living, it does not follow that they should have to cease at once to constitute the British state. On the contrary, so long as the British society has not been incorporated into some other society, whether from the East or from the West, all Englishmen irrespective of their class and creed will have to preserve their independence as a State, cost them what it might. The British State will still have its duty totally unimpaired to preserve the British society. An abeyance of the democratic and autocratic activities in the British society either as a matter of conviction or as the result of invasion from the outside world need not imply the elimination of the British State. The issue of defence and preservation of common interest will still remain to every Conservative and Socialist to account for.

It is another question what such a radical change would imply in practice if all the States on the face of the globe felt called upon to abandon schemes for internal conflicts and concentrate on the one object of preserving the society? Will the States still survive as they are today?

No State will be able to maintain its function as a State as it stands today, since what is common interest and ideal to the citizens of any state is not only in conflict with the common interests and ideals of some other states but, in the last analysis, just a mode of realizing some larger type of common interest. The separate states naturally will be resolved into some larger body since their ideals will cease to be accepted as common.

Even as we stand, the common ideal changes from time to time as we pass from such states as England, Russia or India to societies like Europe or Asia. In other words, when we make the preservation of common interests our main goal rather than the national or racial existence, the scale we choose is on the European or Asian level rather than on the English or Indian or Russian.

To take an instance from recent European history, the common ideal which the notion of Britain symbolizes was in direct conflict with the common ideal which Germany recently represented. And this was so for the simple reason that Germany and England when they were at war with one another, professed the ideal of a larger society, the European. Both of them during the war believed in the European ideal and it may be shown that they were careful enough not to injure the strict European interest. And one may add that in the event of a war between the European and the Asian suddenly breaking out in the midst of the European war, they would have instantly concluded peace and joined together to fight the Asian.

And if the accuracy of this analysis may be open to question from the point of view of technical issues, the point that I am making will not suffer since it does not stand wholly on the basis of the late Anglo-German war. There are unlimited instances which can be produced in evidence of my claim. The truth is that no ideal as we have known it in the history of societies or states can be regarded as the common ideal for the human species, not to say for the universe at large. None of them was an equivalent of the Possibility of the Absolute, although everyone of them claimed to be the sole representative of the ideal of the universe on the ground that it was a direct descent from the mystical absolute or the humanistic infinite. All historical ideals symbolized in the societies and states were illusory, since neither the mystical nor the humanistic ultimates were consistent or comprehensive and they were in perpetual conflict with one another.

What then would happen if the states or societies in at least the known human world wanted to concentrate on the common interests or ideal and ceased to encourage the democratic and autocratic movements?

They would at least have to find out the goal or ideal which is common to all the states and societies by eliminating all the features which created conflicts between them, and firmly to decide not to engage in the precarious art of realizing that ideal. That seems to be the obvious conclusion.

If, however, the inclination to realize the ideal still persists in individuals or groups in spite of the fact that the two ways of realizing it — the democratic and autocratic — are fully accepted as illusory, the way out would be to practise what may be called the "method of abstention" so as to restrain that inclination. Both sides in that case will be called upon to exert themselves to abstain from making efforts to realize the values which created the clash — a procedure which is one form of action just as definite and consistent as the other in which we act to realize the objective.

If, however, the inclinations to realize the values instead of abstaining from realizing it persist, an era will set in, in which the State, while it will concentrate its efforts on working out common interests, will also have to educate the human community in the art of abstention from interests which are sectional, partial and illusory. The two functions of the State: one, that of positive administration in all issues of security and preservation, and two, that of negative preparation either by diverse methods of regulation and education or rigid self-restraint in extremely hard cases will not contradict one another even if they may fall short of ideal excellence.

In any case it will be a truly impartial and a fully representative State. It will not only preserve the whole community irrespective of caste, creed and colour but equally work on behalf of the democrat and autocrat by preaching the ethics of abstention to both in the place of warfare, violent or persuasive. Besides, such a state will leave out the issue of Realization altogether, for the simple reason that it has not yet fallen due. Instead, it will concentrate on cultivating the common interests of the human community or formulating the basic objective of conceiving the main ideal. It will be an advanced State for the following reasons:

> As a State it will for the first time make an effort to conceive the true ideal which still remains unknown in spite of what we have valued as human civilization. There was not a single ideal for which the States have so far worked which could be called real or true and not illusory. Neither the legal nor the moral State had any idea of the real ideal or was even aware that they did not know it.
>
> It will eliminate warfare from human society in both the forms, violent and persuasive.
>
> It will introduce the art of practising mutual abstention in a conflict between values on any plane in the place of warfare. Neither warfare nor persuasion will form its technique or method for any plea or excuse whatever.
>
> If it cannot produce at once the era in which the realization of the ideal can take place, it will have guaranteed its advent by practising rigid abstention from the illusory conceptions of autocracy and democracy.
>
> If realization is postponed, at least false attempts at it are

> eliminated, and a sure mode of paving the way for it is guaranteed. It is this preparation for abstention that will distinguish it pre-eminently from the legal and moral States.

Altogether this State will usher in the era in which at least some clear objectives will be in view:

> A search for the true Ideal, the Possibility of the Absolute, which means almost a religious preparation to come into touch with the "society of beings". This will serve the State as a means of satisfying part of the religious need and instinct of the community — discovery of the Ideal.
>
> Preservation of the species at any cost by avoiding the ominous consequences involved in the perpetual clash between mysticism and humanism, or autocracy and democracy.
>
> Replacement of the destructive methods of violence and persuasion by the method of mutual renunciation and abstention in all matters which created conflict.
>
> Basing the social scheme on as wide a platform as possible and on terms which recognize absolute equality. Absolute equality will not mean democratic equality, whatever its scale or magnitude, nor certainly hierarchy, which is frankly based on humility or inequality. Its objective is neither unity at the cost of freedom, nor uniqueness at the cost of unity. And yet its positive feature appears in a dual form: first, equality with regard to the common interest in spite of differences in caste, creed, colour, age or sex; and second, equality with regard to conflicting interests in the sense of equal obligation to abstain.
>
> Preparation for a period of harmony in which all values and truths will blend; doubt as such will disappear and certainty about the Absolute will prevail.

This is just a broad outline of the State which was directly implied by Gandhiji's comments on history. Neither its main objective nor its technique of mutual abstention has had anything like a requisite formulation in my analysis. Any reader, in consequence, who may still be interested in this new State is bound to raise questions. Besides, the main plank on which the whole theory of this State stands, the "society of beings", the central truth of the message of Gandhi, remains unbuttressed for want of an exposure of the metaphysical bastion which supports it. I did not feel I should support this outline with an elaborate façade of formulation. That is a separate and very difficult function, and I have already partially discharged it elsewhere. The rest will be dealt with in my next book,* at which I have been working since *The Real and the Negative* came out. The critic will be given sufficient evidence for all the issues: the State with its objective and technique, and its bastion, the "society of beings".

In the meantime the least that we can do is to assess the significance of the State which the message from our Bapuji left behind. The time is just ripe for it since by all the evidence it will be a miracle if the State we still cling to does not founder like a ship in the heavy seas. Sooner or later, we shall have to consider a substitute for the State we inherited since it has failed to give us peace, the one thing for which it took from us our loyalty and oath. Particularly for ourselves as Indians it would be an ungracious act if we proceeded to build our State in utter and complete oblivion of Bapuji's message: as if Gandhiji by his life and death assured us that our history or that of our opponent held the final mandate for the constitution of a State. It would be foolhardy to repeat history deliberately, in spite of the collapse of both the historical states, the legal and moral, in the life and death of Bapuji.

But the fact remains that the message has been delivered and nothing that can happen to postpone its fulfilment will

* *Related Mutiplicity*, 1952.

unmake that deliverance. Sooner or later the new state will arise in the human home. My vision on 15 Sravana stands, and it stands confirmed by the message of Bapuji. I feel even more assured that we are on the threshold of peace. This is my humble way of paying tribute to Bapuji who after centuries made our land free and gave us a message after his death about the way of fulfilling the ancestral mandate — peace in the human family with confidence and calm.

Sravana — the 15th

I feel I must record my feelings, for what they are worth, as the dawn breaks after a long night of silence, to bear witness to the rebirth of my ancestry at the tail-end of what has been called the modern age. Perhaps I owe it at least to the younger minds of my country and particularly to the British people with whom I have spent almost the prime of my life and at a period which staged the darkest upheaval in their history — potent enough to reduce any race or pride to despair. And yet there would be no occasion for me to yield even to this call of duty if I had not felt that the rebirth or reawakening of my ancestry in this hour of distress, suspense and confusion is not merely a supreme historic event but a symbol which betokens a future. It is, for certain, in the vivid augury which that symbol holds to me, much more than in its mere immediate presence, that the greatness or significance of the Indian reawakening lies. My heart rejoices in it and I want to share my joy and assurance with all who ever came into my life or worked with me, although apart and aloof, to bring out the light of truth. The symbol to me is one of peace and light which never to my knowledge crossed the threshold of our human home in spite of the efforts of long untold centuries to visualize its form.

Here at last is the sure sign that the long night of history, which spun webs incessantly with the woof of deep disagreements in the human family, is on the wane. There is even evidence that the last battle in the long campaign of warfare between the Mystic and the Humanist is at an end.

Neither the Legal nor the Moral State nor the values which held to the joy of abnegation or to its definite opposite, unrestricted enjoyment of self, need any longer be looking for fresh grounds to renew or repeat the attempt to dominate the human mind. There should be room instead from now on for faith and action which, it is expected, will resolve the disagreements and bring a new foundation to our social home. Most decidedly, it is not the moment for the meek who surrender human dignity nor for the sceptic who claims unreservedly to dictate.

And the secret of this endeavour to build up a new society with a state which does not derive either from its moral or legal ancestry will look for its inspiration from the heart of the universe — the unity and agreement which literally gave birth to it. There is evidence for the assurance that there is somewhere a society of beings in the universe which holds aloft the ideal about which there can be no disagreement. And, to me, the clear indication of the Indian symbol is that this society, however unknown to or unfelt by historic tradition, is a fact and stands upon the essential unity and energy behind any movement that ever took place.

I am not, however, raising any occult or legendary issue, or one which is merely speculative and mystical. What is persistent and uppermost in me at the moment is a feeling that I should assure all those who will read this note that a moment has arrived in our history for the statesman and the jurist to lay the foundation of a new society or State which will depart equally from the legal and the moral states of our tradition. And this assurance comes to me not as a matter of mere feeling but as a result of patient and long analysis, a part of which has already seen the light of day. Some at least of my contemporaries are familiar with it. I am convinced that it does not mean a mere Asian leadership, nor a leadership of the world in the sense the European even now takes it to mean or our ancestors in their non-political way realized in the ancient past. It means leadership in founding a World State the structure of which will not be shaped in the form of the Legal or Moral State, leadership which in the nature of things cannot be restricted to race, region or creed. To me, definitely, the rebirth of the Indian ancestry has a twofold significance. It is a commentary on the past of all ancestries to the effect that it was a closed epoch in which warfare by violence or expansion by persuasion produced nothing but discipline for the human species, and a distinct augury that the era of construction and peace on the basis of the eternal agreements behind the deep disagreements of history is at hand. Personally, I feel that the world at large may forthwith proceed to materialize this augury and write off the two old techniques of violence and persuasion as outworn and obsolete. At any rate, with my experience both about my ancestry and that of the European, it is not possible that I should miss the meaning of the symbol which the rebirth of the Indian mind so clearly indicates. It is my earnest hope that it will not be long before my contemporaries see it. I feel confident that human history, unfolding the pages of the two major conflicts — that between the Group and the Individualist societies and that between the Authoritarian and the Libertarian outlook — in the course of at least 5,000 years, stands today in the deep embrace of its last and final stage of impasse and confusion. The alternatives, therefore, are a conflagration in which the universe itself might go up in smoke and the beginning of a new epoch of history in which the conflicting values and schemes will find a common field in which to work out their distinctive ends. Not even the prospect of compromise can create a diversion. The rebirth of my ancestry heralds the rejuvenation of human society and rules out the dire prospect of the extinction of our species. One feels one cannot help being prophetic in the presence of such a reawakening. And what revitalizes this faith and makes it almost scientific certainty for me is the result of my own analysis which is remote and distant from any tradition. I have no alternative but to paint the augury of my ancestral rebirth as the future of our race. If we do not mean to leave this earth, our ancestral home, for good and all, we should proceed sooner than we can think to build the foundation of that home or the World State. I am sure this is no offence to any racial pride nor the least curtailment of human hopes.